Physical Characteristics of the Finnish Spitz

(from the American Kennel Club bree

Body: Muscular, square.

Tail: Set on just below level of topline, forming a single curl falling over the loin with tip pointing towards the thigh. Plumed, curving vigorously from its base in an arch forward, downward, and backward.

Hindquarters: Angulation in balance with the forequarters. *Thighs*—Muscular. *Hocks*—Moderately let down. Straight and parallel.

Coat: The coat is double with a short, soft, dense undercoat and long, harsh straight guard hairs measuring approximately one to two inches on the body. Hair on the head and legs is short and close; it is longest and most dense on plume of tail and back of thighs.

Size: Height at the withers in dogs, 17 to 20 inches; in bitches, 15 to 18 inches.

Feet: Rounded, compact foot with well-arched toes, tightly bunched or close-cupped, the two center toes being only slightly longer than those on the outside.

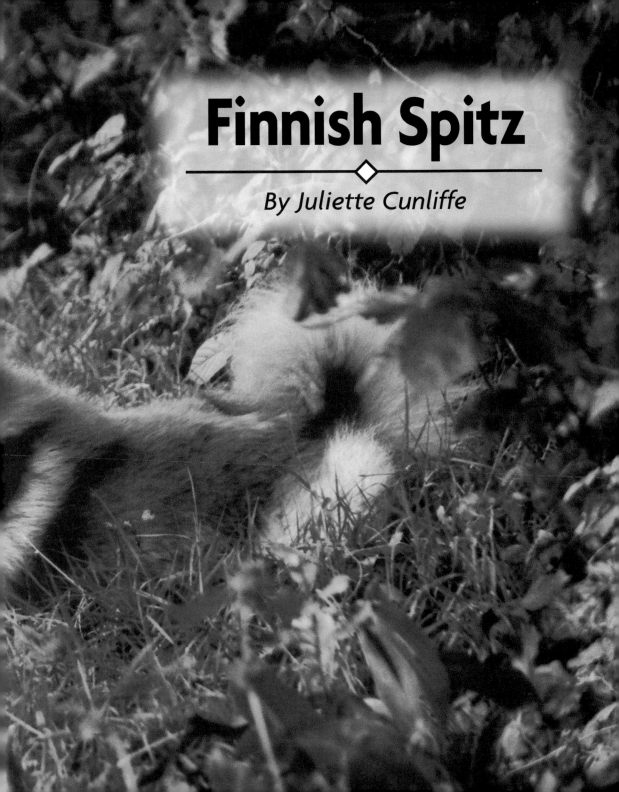

Finnish Spitz

◇

By Juliette Cunliffe

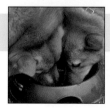

Contents

KENNEL CLUB BOOKS: **FINNISH SPITZ**
ISBN: 1-59378-361-2

Copyright © 2003 Kennel Club Books, Inc.
308 Main Street, Allenhurst, NJ 07711 USA
Cover Design Patented: US 6,435,559 B2 • Printed in South Korea

Photographs by Carol Ann Johnson, with additional photos by:
Norvia Behling, T.J. Calhoun, Carolina Biological Supply, Juliette Cunliffe, Doskocil, Isabelle Francais, James Hayden-Yoav, James R. Hayden, RBP, Bill Jonas, Dwight R. Kuhn, Dr. Dennis Kunkel, Mikki Pet Products, Phototake, Jean Claude Revy, Dr. Andrew Spielman and Alice van Kempen.

The publisher would like to thank all of the owners of the dogs featured in this book, including Debbie Coe and Jo Mansfield.

Illustrations by Patricia Peters.

Here comes the Finnish Spitz! Quick, alert, and keen only begin to describe this "foxy" national dog of Finland, a prized working bird dog in its native land.

HISTORY OF THE

FINNISH SPITZ

The Finnish Spitz is the national dog of Finland, its ancestors having been brought there from Russia by tribes of Finno-Ugrian peoples around 100 AD. Some of the tribes settled in isolated areas in the far north of Finland, and, of course, they took their dogs with them. So it was that in northern Finland, Lapland and the settlements of the Finnish tribes in Russian Karelia, an all-purpose hunting dog developed that was to become the Finnish Spitz.

In Finland, the breed is called the Suomenpystykorva, or the Finnish Cock-Eared Dog, though it has also been known as the Finnish Barking Bird Dog. Unfortunately, there is little reliable data about the early history of the breed in Finland, but some old documents have indeed proved the early existence of such dogs. Wilhelm von Wright mentioned a "foxlike bird dog" in 1834 and, in 1875, the French explorer de la Martiniere mentioned deep red dogs that he had encountered even as far north as the Muurmanni coast.

It is likely that the hunting tribesmen who lived around the

SPITZ ANCESTORS

The ancestors of the European spitz group of dogs can be traced back to the hunter-gatherers of the Stone Age, some 6,000 years ago. The Turf Spitz was a dog buried by accident and preserved in the peat bogs that ranged from the northern plains of Germany through most of Denmark. Because this was an area of swampland, houses were built on stilts. Over time, well-preserved remains of humans as well as dogs have been recovered from the resultant peat bogs.

central area of the Volga River obtained their dogs from others within their own group or from those living nearby. However, when some of the Finns from this area began their migration toward the Baltic Sea, they were in contact with German and Baltic people for a long while. Thus, their dogs underwent conformational changes, a natural result of having been mixed with Middle-European breeds.

When tribes moved northward, though, to find better hunting grounds, they took with them their dogs, which had already been developed for this very purpose. They were smaller than the dogs from the Finno-Ugric age, for their usage was now rather different. There were fewer game animals about, so the ability to hold prey at bay and kill prey had become less important than scenting ability, tracking skills and the ability to inform the master. The Finnish Spitz had become a highly useful dog but, in the remote areas of Finland, where the dogs had remained fairly pure-bred, they had to find their own food, too. Here they hunted birds and small animals, and they tended to stay close to people's houses to seek protection from wolves. Indeed the Finnish Spitz's battle for survival was a tough one.

FEAR FOR THE BREED'S SURVIVAL

By the 1880s, the pure-bred Finnish Spitz found itself virtually on the edge of extinction. Thankfully, though, two foresters, Hugo Richard Sandberg and Hugo Roos, decided to do what they could to save the breed, for they realized just how serious the situation was.

Hugo Sandberg wrote about the breed in *Sporten* magazine in 1890, saying how the Finnish dog lived in close contact with his family and shared with them both "the sunny and the cloudy days." He talked of the dog's displays of devotion and "self-sacrificing loyalty" toward his master and wrote that the dog had a lot more courage than one would expect

from such a small breed.

Indeed this was a highly important article, for in it Mr. Sandberg also suggested that the Finnish Kennel Club, which had only been formed in 1889, should restore this valuable and truly native breed. According to the club's rules, it was bound to "promote better caretaking of dogs in our country (Finland) by spreading general information about pure-bred dogs and the advantages of breeding pure-bred dogs."

Thus it was that in 1892, the Finnish Spitz as we know it today was included in the Finnish Kennel Club's stud book, and the standard for the breed's conformation as suggested by Mr. Sandberg was approved. Shows were held and the breed took its fair share of prizes at these events. In 1897, the standard was revised and the breed's name officially became Finnish Spitz. Hugo Roos was an active breeder for 30 years and exhibited for even longer. It was he who played the major part in gathering the foundation stock of the breed for its reestablishment.

A SPITZ BY ANY OTHER NAME...

Over the years, the Finnish Spitz has come to be known by a number of different names: Suomenpystykorva, Suomalainen Pistykorven, Finnish Cock-Eared Dog, Finnish Hunting Dog, Barking Bird Dog, Finsk Spets, Finnish Spets or Loulou Finois (or Finlandais). In Count Henri Bylandt's book, published in the Netherlands in 1894, the names Finnish Pom and Finsche Keeshond were also included. Affectionate nicknames are "Finkie" or "Finsky."

THE 20th CENTURY IN FINLAND

Until the 1920s, Hugo Roos was considered the pioneer of the breed, which has continued to increase in popularity over the years. In 1925, the breed standard was again revised, and it remained the same until another revision in 1996. In 1979, the Finnish Spitz was declared Finland's national breed, this being a fine reward for the efforts put forth by the breed's loyal enthusiasts over preceding decades. It is significant that in Finland's show rings today, no Finnish Spitz may claim the title of champion without having gained a working or trials certificate, thus underlining the dedication to preserving the breed's original and true characteristics.

HUNTING IN FINLAND

In Finland, the breed is very much a working animal, having been used for centuries by huntsmen to hunt forest game. Their prey has included elk, bear, squirrel and hare, as well as the game birds cappercaillie and grouse. Working with the Finnish Spitz always demands a sure-footed hunter for the varied terrain, ranging from moss-covered boulders to marshland.

Today the Finnish Spitz is primarily kept in rural regions where game is used to feed the families of the huntsmen, though hunting is only allowed during the specified hunting season, and the number of birds taken is strictly regulated. In fact, in years when numbers of cappercaillie are low, Finnish Kennel Club registration figures for the breed decline accordingly. This breed is also used as a guard, for the Finnish Spitz can be highly vocal.

It is believed that, in Finland, birds were hunted using traps even as late as the 1930s. Therefore, the Finnish Spitz has only been used as a barking bird dog from that time on. However, the method of hunting employed with the Finnish Spitz is very specific to this breed. The dog is trained to range ahead of the hunter and, when quarry (a bird) is found, the bird is followed until it settles in a tree. The dog runs then forward and backward, swaying his tail. These actions attract the bird's attention and lull it into a false sense of security. Some say that the bird feels as if it is being confronted by a swaying serpent, and, mesmerized, it follows the dog with its gaze, giving the hunter the opportunity to move in closer to take his shot.

The Finnish Spitz then barks, becoming increasingly louder. The dog's noise, often referred to as yodeling, camouflages that of the approaching hunter, who takes an accurate shot at the bird. However, there are occasions when the bird moves off before the hunter has reached a suitable position for a shot, in which case the dog stops barking and once more begins to track the bird until it settles again.

THE FINNISH SPITZ REACHES BRITAIN

Although there may possibly have been a handful of Finnish Spitzen brought to Britain beforehand, it was in 1920 that Sir Edward Chichester became attracted to the breed while on a hunting trip in Finland. He brought a brace (pair) over to Britain and later an unrelated stud dog. Another person who had seen the breed in Finland and imported dogs was Lady Kitty Ritson (Tulchan). It was she who, with Mrs. de la Poer Beresford (Whiteway), Lionel Taylor (Hello), Mrs. and Miss Pink (later Mrs. Piper) and Mrs.

Hallo Aaro Ukinpoika, owned by Mr. L. S. Taylor, has a head and expression typical of dogs shown in the 1930s. Some examples of that time were even more fox-like in appearance.

A Hungarian-owned Finnish Spitz of the 1930s. This dog's head construction is quite different than other breed representatives of the day, and certainly different than the dogs of today.

A reproduction of a painting by Dorothy Hallett, showing Rusty, an import owned by Sir Edward Chichester, who is generally credited with the breed's popularity in the UK. In the early days, the breed was known as "Finsk Spets" in Britain.

Moulton (Boydon), set up the Finnish Spitz Club, which was registered with the English Kennel Club in 1934.

During the first few years, the imported dogs allowed the breed to become established in Britain, but, as with so many breeds, the Finnish Spitz encountered serious problems with the onset of World War II. Thankfully, the imports, Mountjay Peter, Kiho Seivi and, from Sweden, Friedstahills Saila, helped the breed enormously, and others of value followed them. Tophunter Tommi and Tophunter Turre were born in quarantine and, as the years went on, they appeared in the vast majority of the pedigrees of the UK's most successful dogs.

Tommi and Turre were later owned by Mrs. Griselda Price (Cullabine), who was the importer of Kiho Tipsa. Her stock was largely founded on Lady Kitty Ritson's Tulchans and

LANGUAGE LESSON
The Finno-Ugrian group of languages includes Finnish, Estonian, Lapp and Hungarian, as well as some other north-eastern European languages. About 22 million people speak one of the languages classified within this group.

she also became the owner of Una of Snowland, another Finnish Spitz to appear in many of the breed's successful pedigrees. More recently, it is Eng. Ch. Urheilu Pennan Pipsa of Toveri who has dominated top-winning pedigrees; she also is the breed's top brood bitch of all time.

THE BREED ARRIVES IN THE US

It is believed that the first Finnish Spitz to arrive in the US was Cullabine Rudolph, who was sent there from Griselda Price's Cullabine kennels in 1959. Breeding of Finnish Spitzen in the

Tommi and his sire Hammon, two remarkable Finnish Spitzen owned by Sir Edward Chichester.

A well-known and respected British dog breeder and judge, Lady Kitty Ritson, pictured with a Finnish Spitz. She was one of the first to import the breed into the UK and was a specialist on the breed.

US did not, however, begin until the mid-1960s, this with the use of imports from Finland, owned by Henry Davidson of Minnesota and Alex Hassel of Connecticut.

In 1975, the Finnish Spitz Club of America was formed and, a year later, the breed standard was drawn up, based on that used in Finland. Not until 1983 was the Finnish Spitz accepted into the American Kennel Club's Miscellaneous Class, and the breed was approved to be shown in this class beginning in April 1984. AKC Stud Book registrations for the breed commenced in 1987.

On January 1, 1988, the Finnish Spitz became eligible to compete at AKC-licensed shows in the Non-Sporting Group and, in 1992, the breed club held its first national specialty in Tulsa, Oklahoma. The Finnish Spitz Club of America was doubtless proud to become a member club of the AKC in 1993. This is the national parent club for the breed, and it is dedicated to encouraging and promoting the breeding of pure-bred Finnish Spitzen, doing all that is possible to bring the breed's natural qualities to a state of perfection.

THE FINNISH SPITZ ON POSTAGE STAMPS
Despite its being a breed that is not especially well known, the Finnish Spitz appears on a number of postage stamps and

other collectible items. In 1965, Finland produced a set of stamps that included the Karelian Bear Dog, the Hamiltonstövare and, of course, the Finnish Spitz. They were printed from line-engraved plates, such that the printing ink was held in the lines scratched onto the smooth surface of a printing plate, made either of steel or copper. This is known as the intaglio process, and was the method used for the famous "Penny Black" stamp. What is of special interest is that 1965 was indeed rather late to still be using this early printing process, and so adds to the interest of this trio of Finnish stamps.

Another highly interesting aspect of this particular set of stamps is that it was one of the first sets of stamps to carry a surcharge, something that was subsequently donated to a charity, in this case the Anti-TB Fund.

Another set of Finnish stamps depicting dogs was issued in 1989. This time the stamps featured the three breeds already mentioned, plus the Finnish Lapphund. This was to commemorate the 100th anniversary of the Finnish Kennel Club and was

The Finnish Spitz Noita. It was noted that this dog represented what the breed should look like in the 1930s, and that while the Finnish Spitz cannot be mistaken for any other breed, it is undeniable that the breed belongs to the spitz ("spitz" meaning "pointed" in German) family.

very different than the first set of stamps, for it was a mini-sheet of stamps with the design continuing onto the border.

The third set of Finnish dog stamps was issued in 1998 to coincide with the hosting of the World Dog Show. This time, there were eight stamps in booklet form, but how disappointed Finnish Spitz enthusiasts must have been to find that the only Finnish breed included was the Lapphund.

THE BREED IN OTHER COUNTRIES

The Finnish Spitz has been imported in small numbers to many countries throughout the world. In 1952, it found its way to the Netherlands, where it was introduced into the county by J. W. H. Scholtens-Keyzer. In Canada, the breed arrived in the early 1970s; by 1974, there was sufficient interest in the Finnish Spitz for it to be accepted by the Canadian Kennel Club.

A modern champion Finnish Spitz, showing the breed's type today.

CHARACTERISTICS OF THE

FINNISH SPITZ

There is a lot to love about this intelligent, attractive red dog, which is both a hunter and a family companion, sometimes affectionately known as "Finkie." With his acute hearing, the Finnish Spitz is an excellent watchdog, but more of an alarm dog than a guard dog; although he barks, he rarely bites. This is a relatively small breed, yet it is usually said that the Finnish Spitz has the temperament and character of a much larger dog.

Although he comes from Nordic regions, he seems to adapt fairly easily to both heat and cold. He needs a good deal of exercise, but the Finnish Spitz is more than willing to lie down in a comfortable place with his human family at the end of the day. He should, however, never be considered a lap dog.

FOXY!
The Finnish Spitz is often likened to a fox. This is due in part to his fox-like head, but also to his rich red color. Some think that the expression "bright-eyed and bushy-tailed" might just have been coined to describe the Finnish Spitz.

PERSONALITY

The Finnish Spitz is a lively dog that is very alert and can be wonderfully playful, making a great family companion for all ages. This is not a breed that adapts well to a strictly kenneled living situation; he needs time both outdoors for exercise and indoors as a part of his family's life.

The Finnish Spitz is friendly and wants both affection and attention, but is independent and can be rather aloof with strangers. The nature of the Finnish Spitz is somewhat protective and the breed does establish a dominance hierarchy, with males tending to be rather domineering and dog-aggressive. Having said that, though, most Finnish Spitzen do get along well with other dogs in the home.

The Finnish Spitz is a playful dog that generally loves the company of children. However, young children and dogs should always be supervised when together. Even though the breed is not really a large one, accidents can happen. Also, the coat can be pulled, and toddlers can often be quite rough in their games. Children of all ages must be taught to treat dogs kindly, gently and with respect.

This is quite a sensitive breed; harsh discipline is not at all suitable for a Finnish Spitz. Patience and understanding are musts, and any training given must be consistent. It is important that puppies are taught what they are and are not allowed to do early on, because, if given half the chance, they will take over the household.

This is a breed that, because of its intelligence, has the capability of learning quickly. However, also because of the breed's intelligence, Finnish Spitzen can get incredibly bored if required to repeat things too often! Some are trained for the lower levels of obedience competition but, as with all breeds that are not reputed to be top obedience material, there can be exceptions and some Finnish Spitzen fare well at the higher levels.

This is also a breed that likes to keep clean, and they always seem happy to wash each other as well as themselves!

THE FINNISH SPITZ AND HIS BARK

Finnish Spitzen, like the majority of spitz breeds, have vociferous

SPITZ BREEDS

The word "spitz" is a general word used to describe dogs with pointed ears and sharp muzzles. The spitz breeds also all have curled tails and dense, double coats. The Finnish Spitz is one of many spitz breeds found today in show rings around the world.

Another of the spitz family, the German Spitz.

HUNTING AND ESCAPING

Finnish Spitzen seem to have an inclination to hunt anything that moves, which, after all, is their natural instinct. Good sturdy fencing is therefore essential around the perimeter of your property, and you should check the fence regularly to make sure that your canine hunter does not have an escape route!

barks, which need to be kept under control. Working dogs in their homeland are taught to bark at certain game, while ignoring other birds and animals. Since the Finnish Spitz is a breed that was developed to bark, owners must be aware that barking is a part of the dog's nature. With correct training, barking can be controlled, and it is essential that your Spitz knows without a doubt that excessive barking will not be tolerated. Constant barking can be a dreadful nuisance both to you and, more importantly, to your neighbors.

When kept outside, especially for long periods, a Finnish Spitz will be inclined to bark at every new event, and he has a range of other vocalizations, too. In Scandinavia, official competitions are held to find the "King of the Barkers." It is worth bearing in mind that in barking contests held in Finland, the Finnish Spitz has been known to bark as many as 160 times in a minute!

A breeder and his Finnish pack. Although the breed generally gets along well with its housemates, owning a group of these assertive dogs is certainly a big responsibility.

PHYSICAL CHARACTERISTICS

The whole appearance of this bold spitz breed indicates his liveliness, something that shines through especially in his eyes, ears and tail, the latter of which is plumed and curved vigorously from its root, in an arch but not in a full circle. The breed standard explains exactly how the tail of the Finnish Spitz should lie.

There should be no suggestion of coarseness in this compact dog, which has a body that is almost square in outline. It is generally accepted, though, that bitches can be a little longer in body than dogs. The chest is deep and the belly just slightly drawn up. The feet are preferably round and, although removal of front dewclaws is optional, hind ones must always be removed.

The Finnish Spitz is a hard-conditioned hunting dog with medium bone and strong hindquarters, but only a moderate turn of stifle and medium angulation of hock. The neck of the Finnish Spitz is somewhat shorter than that found in some of the other spitz breeds. This is coupled with the fact that the shoulders are somewhat straighter than in many other breeds, because the breed points upward when working.

NATURE LOVER

Many Finnish Spitzen enjoy a good romp in the snow and some have quite a passion for barking at snowflakes. The Finnish Spitz can also be a very good mouser and loves all of Nature's little adventures.

TOO MUCH STARCH

Skin problems in dogs can be caused by feeding too many treats, especially if those seemingly enjoyable snacks contain too much starch. A well-balanced diet will often deal with the problem, bringing skin and coat condition back to normal once again.

HEAD AND EARS

The medium-sized head is clean-cut, longer than it is broad, and the forehead is slightly arched. There is a moderate stop, and the muzzle tapers so that, when seen from above and from the sides, it tapers evenly. The black lips are thin and tightly closed, and the jaws are strong with a scissors bite. The nose is deep black; sometimes the Finnish Spitz is referred to as *pikinokka*, which means "pitch-black nose" in Finnish.

The medium-sized, almond-shaped eyes are preferably dark, and they must be lively. Here, pigment is again important, for the eye rims must be black. The eyes are set on a slight slant, the outer corners tilted upward. The small, cocked ears are sharply pointed, being fine in texture and mobile. All of the aspects of the head join together to give the Finnish Spitz a thoroughly expressive face, one that is indeed capable of showing a range of emotions. Something also very important in this breed is that dogs should have a masculine appearance about the head and bitches should be clearly feminine.

SIZE

Although not a large breed, males are generally considerably larger than females, and males carry more coat. In Finland, dogs that are not within the size limits are penalized, but standards of some

Left: A well-shaped head with the characteristic tapering muzzle, black nose, dark eyes and black pigmentation. Right: The high-set ears are small, pointed and mobile, standing upward over the eyes when alert.

This Finnish Spitz and his Shetland Sheepdog pal are right at home, making themselves comfortable and sharing some quiet time.

other countries place more emphasis on balance and proportions.

Dogs stand 17–20 inches (43–51 cm) at the withers, while bitches are 15–18 inches (38–46 cm). The weight range is not specified in the AKC standard, but the British standard indicates that the weight should be from 14–16 kg (31–35 lb). There should be plenty of air space beneath the chest.

MOVEMENT
The Finnish Spitz has a light, springy gait, which is both quick and graceful. The breed's function in its homeland should always be borne in mind when considering its movement, and there should be drive from behind when on the move.

COAT AND COLOR
The red color of the Finnish Spitz is highly attractive to the eye. The color should preferably be bright on the back, of a reddish-brown or red-gold. Hairs in other places, as specified in the breed standard, are of lighter shades, as is the undercoat. Together these shades give a "glow" to the visual appearance of the coat.

INFECTION AID
At the first sign of any minor infection, the author has often found that live yogurt, administered orally, is of great benefit. This sometimes has the effect of rectifying the problem almost immediately, before a course of antibiotics becomes necessary.

Puppies may have some black hair, but these decrease with age. The breed standard clearly describes the limited amount of black hair that is permitted in the breed as a whole.

The type of coat on the Finnish Spitz is very typical of other spitz breeds, with a short, soft, dense undercoat and an outer coat of semi-erect, stiffer, longer hair. On the head and front of the legs, the hair is short and close, but it is longer and coarser elsewhere. The outer coat on the shoulders is considerably longer and coarser, and the ruff around the neck is more prominent in dogs than in bitches. On the back of the thighs and on the tail, the hair is longer and more dense. No trimming is allowed on this breed, not even of the whiskers.

HEALTH CONSIDERATIONS

In general, the Finnish Spitz is a very healthy dog. It is reported that, out of all breeds, this breed has one of the lowest frequencies of hip dysplasia and progressive retinal atrophy (PRA); both of these problems are found frequently in many breeds. However, certain health issues can arise, so it is in the best interests of the breed if new and prospective owners know what to look out for. If owners are aware of the problems that can occur, they are undoubtedly in a position to deal with them in the best manner possible. Some are genetic and are carried via heredity, while others are not.

DEHYDRATION

Some Finnish Spitzen seem rather susceptible to dehydration when they suffer from an illness. In such cases, the use of a drip can be very beneficial.

OBESITY

Because Finnish Spitzen, as a breed, use their food very efficiently, they do not normally eat great quantities. Thus, they can have a tendency to gain weight quickly if they are overfed. It is therefore prudent to pay careful attention to your dog's weight, for a dog carrying excess weight tends to be less healthy than one of the correct weight for his breed.

TEETH

It is important to pay close attention to the care of your Finnish Spitz's teeth and gums so that they remain as healthy as possible, thereby preventing decay, infection and resultant loss. If infection is evident in the gums, always deal with it promptly, for the infection may not just stop there. The bacteria can be carried through the bloodstream, the result of which can be disease of the liver, kidneys, heart and joints. This is all the more reason to realize that efficient dental care is of utmost importance throughout a dog's life.

Feeding dry foods is recommended by many as a means of helping to keep a dog's teeth clean and in good condition. Of course, regular, careful brushing with a veterinary toothpaste can help enormously and should be a part of your Finnish Spitz's routine care. You can incorporate his tooth-cleaning into his grooming sessions.

ALLERGIES

Dogs of any breed can suffer from an allergy. Allergies can often be kept under control with a carefully considered diet. An allergy may be noticed by the appearance of "hot spots" on the skin, despite there being no sign of external parasites. A low-protein diet often seems to suit skin troubles.

It is often extremely difficult to ascertain the cause of a dog's allergy, because it can be caused by a number of things. The many possibilities range from the living room carpet, the shampoo used

SAMPLE TIP
To take a urine sample to your vet for analysis, the easiest way is to catch the urine in a large, clean bowl and then transfer it to a bottle. Owners attempting to get their dogs or bitches to urinate directly into bottles will spend many fruitless hours in their efforts.

when bathing and, quite frequently, certain grasses and molds. In cases of skin allergy, it is a good idea to change the type of shampoo, conditioning rinse and any coat sprays used, for these are perhaps the easiest items to eliminate before looking further, if necessary. It goes without saying that your Finnish Spitz must be kept free of all external parasites.

EYE INFECTIONS

Always be sure to keep an eye on the cleanliness and condition of your Finnish Spitz's eyes, so as to avoid the occurrence of eye infections. At the first sign of injury, especially if the eye is starting to turn blue in color, urgent veterinary attention is required. Early diagnosis and treatment can often save a dog's sight.

HEART PROBLEMS

Occasionally, dogs can suffer from heart problems, particularly as they become more advanced in

age. It is therefore sensible to request that the vet check your dog's heart whenever you visit his office for any reason. Many good veterinarians will do this automatically, and heart checks certainly should be a part of all routine physical exams.

HEAT EXHAUSTION

Any breed of dog can suffer from heat exhaustion and frequently people do not realize how quickly death can result. The first sign is heavy panting, and the dog begins to puff or gasp for air. When walk-ing, the dog appears dizzy and tends to weave, subsequently collapsing and eventually becom-ing unconscious.

At the first sign, the dog should be taken out of the sun and offered water. The dog's body should be doused with water, especially the head and neck. If available, ice bags or even a pack-age of frozen vegetables should be placed around the dog's head and neck. Because it is urgently neces-sary to lower the dog's tempera-ture, it should be done even before taking your dog to the vet.

Your Finnish Spitz needs and enjoys time outdoors, but be aware of things like potential grass and pollen allergies, as well as heat exhaustion. Remember that the breed is designed for survival in the cold northern climates.

INTRODUCTION TO THE BREED STANDARD

In the United States, the breed standard for each breed is created by the breed's national parent club and then submitted to the American Kennel Club for approval. Standards can be changed occasionally, with such changes coming about with guidance from experienced people within the breed club.

All breed standards are designed effectively to paint a picture in words, with this picture showing an ideal representative of a given breed. Each reader, however, will almost certainly have a slightly different way of interpreting the words and envisioning the picture. After all, were everyone to interpret a breed's standard in exactly the same way, there would only be one consistent winner within the breed at any given time!

A breed standard guides breeders in producing stock that comes as close as possible to the ideal set forth in the breed standard, and helps judges to know exactly what they are looking for in the show ring. This enables each judge to make a carefully considered decision when selecting the most typical specimen present to head his line of winners.

In any event, to fully comprehend the intricacies of a breed, reading words alone is never enough. In addition, it is essential for devotees to watch Finnish Spitzen being judged at shows and, if possible, to attend seminars at which the breed is discussed. This enables owners to absorb as much as possible about the breed. "Hands-on" experience, providing an opportunity to assess the structure of dogs, is always

Head study in profile showing correct type, balance and structure with a mature coat.

In addition to the overall fox-like appearance, distinct traits of the breed include the curled tail, dense coat seen in shades of rich red-gold and the undeniably spitz head with pointed ears and muzzle.

valuable, especially for those who hope ultimately to judge the breed.

However familiar you are with the Finnish Spitz, it is always worth refreshing your memory by reading and re-reading the standard, for it is sometimes all too easy to overlook, or perhaps to conveniently forget, certain features.

THE AMERICAN KENNEL CLUB BREED STANDARD FOR THE FINNISH SPITZ

General Appearance: The Finnish Spitz presents a fox-like picture. The breed has long been used to hunt small game and birds. The pointed muzzle, erect ears, dense coat and curled tail denotes its northern heritage. The Finnish Spitz's whole being shows liveliness, which is especially evident in the eyes, ears and tail. Males are decidedly masculine without coarseness. Bitches are decidedly feminine without over-refinement. The Finnish Spitz's most important characteristics are its square, well-balanced body that is symmetrical with no exaggerated features, a glorious red-gold coat, his bold carriage and brisk movement. Any deviation from the ideal described standard should be penalized to the extent of the

deviation. Structural faults common to all breeds are as undesirable in the Finnish Spitz as in any other breed, even though such faults may not be mentioned in the standard.

Size, Proportion, Substance: *Size*—Height at the withers in dogs, 17 to 20 inches; in bitches, 15 to 18 inches. *Proportion*— Square: length from forechest to buttocks equal to height from withers to ground. The coat may distort the square appearance. *Substance*—Substance and bone in proportion to overall dog.

Head: Clean cut and fox-like. Longer from occiput to tip of nose than broad at widest part of skull in a ratio of 7:4. More refined with less coat or ruff in females than in males, but still in the same ratio. A muscular or coarse head, or a long or narrow head with snipy muzzle, is to be penalized. *Expression*—Fox-like and lively.

Eyes—Almond-shaped with black rims. Obliquely set with moderate spacing between, neither too far apart nor too close. Outer corners tilted upward. Dark in color with a keen and alert expression. Any deviation, runny, weepy, round or light eyes should be faulted. *Ears*—Set on high. When alert, upward standing, open to the front with tips directly above the outer corner of the eyes. Small erect, sharply pointed and very mobile. Ears set too high, too low, or too close together, long or excessive hair inside the ears are faults. *Skull*—Flat between ears with some minimal rounding ahead of earset. Forehead a little arched. Skull to muzzle ratio 4:3. *Stop*—Pronounced. *Muzzle*—Narrow as seen from the front, above and the side; of equal width and depth where it insets to the skull, tapering somewhat, equally from all angles. *Nose*—Black. Any deviation is to be penalized. Circumference of the nose to be 80% of the circumference of the muzzle at its origin. *Lips*—Black; thin and tight. *Bite*—Scissors bite. Wry mouth is to be severely faulted.

Neck, Topline, Body: *Neck*—Well set, muscular. Clean, with no excess skin below the muzzle. Appearing shorter in males due to their heavier ruff. *Topline*—Level and strong from withers to croup. *Body*—Muscular, square. *Chest*—

FAULTS IN PROFILE

Head coarse and heavy, short thick neck, loaded upright shoulders, too high on leg, lacking sufficient angulation behind.

Ewe-necked, upright shoulders, weak narrow front, toes out, low tail set, lacking sufficient angulation behind, low on leg.

Short thick neck, thick upright shoulders, long backed, high in the rear, foreface too long and weak underjaw, lacking sufficient angulation behind.

Short ewe-neck, upright shoulders, soft topline, fine boned, flat feet, lacking sufficient angulation behind.

Deep, reaches to below the elbow. Ratio of chest depth to distance from withers to ground is 4:9. *Ribs*—Well sprung. *Tuck-up*—Slightly drawn up. *Loin*—Short. *Tail*—Set on just below level of topline, forming a single curl falling over the loin with tip pointing towards the thigh. Plumed, curving vigorously from its base in an arch forward, downward, and backward, pressing flat against either thigh with tip extending to middle part of thigh. When straightened, the tip of the tailbone reaches the hock joint. Low or high tail-set, too curly a tail, or a short tail is to be faulted.

Forequarters: *Shoulders*—The layback of the shoulders is 30 degrees to the vertical. *Legs*—Viewed from the front, moderately spaced, parallel and straight with elbows close to the body and turned neither out nor in. Bone strong without being heavy, always in proportion to the dog. Fine bone, which limits endurance, or heavy bone, which makes working movement cumbersome, is to be faulted. *Pasterns*—Viewed from the side, slope slightly. Weak pasterns are to be penalized. *Dewclaws*—May be removed. *Feet*—Rounded, compact foot with well-arched toes, tightly bunched or close-cupped, the two center toes being only slightly longer than those on the outside. The toe pads should be deeply cushioned and covered with thick skin. The impression left by such a foot is rounded in contrast to oval.

Hindquarters: Angulation in balance with the forequarters. *Thighs*—Muscular. *Hocks*—Moderately let down. Straight and parallel. *Dewclaws*—Removed. *Feet*—As in front.

Coat: The coat is double with a short, soft, dense undercoat and long, harsh straight guard hairs measuring approximately 1 to 2 inches on the body. Hair on the head and legs is short and close; it is longest and most dense on plume of tail and back of thighs. The outer coat is stiffer and longer on the neck and back, and in males considerably more profuse at the shoulder, giving them a more ruffed appearance. Males carry more coat than females. No trimming of the coat except for feet is allowed. Whiskers shall not be trimmed. Any trimming of coat shall be severely faulted. Silky, wavy, long or short coat is to be faulted.

Color: Varying shades of golden-red ranging from pale honey to deep auburn are allowed, with no preference given to shades at either extreme so long as the color is bright and clear. As the undercoat is a paler color, the effect of this shading is a coat which appears to glow. White markings on the tips of the toes and a quarter-sized spot or narrow white strip, ideally no wider than 1 inch, on the forechest are permitted. Black hairs along lipline and sparse, separate black hairs on tail and back permitted. Puppies may have a good many black hairs which decrease with age, black on tail persisting longer. Muddy or unclear color, any white on the body except as specified, is to be penalized.

Gait: The Finnish Spitz is quick and light on his feet, steps out briskly, trots with lively grace, and tends to single-track as the speed increases. When hunting, he moves at a gallop. The angulation called for permits him to break into a working gait quickly. Sound movement is essential for stamina and agility.

Temperament: Active and friendly, lively and eager, faithful; brave, but cautious. Shyness, any tendency toward unprovoked aggression is to be penalized.

Note: Finnish Spitz are to be examined on the ground.

Approved July 12, 1999
Effective August 30, 1999

In motion, the Finnish Spitz should be quick, graceful and light on his feet.

FINNISH SPITZ

SELECTING A BREEDER AND PUPPY

Before reaching the decision that you will begin your search for a Finnish Spitz puppy, it is essential that you are certain that the Finnish Spitz is absolutely the most suitable breed for you and your family. You should have carefully researched the breed prior to your decision that a Finnish Spitz should join you and your family in your daily life.

Once you have made the decision that the Finnish Spitz is the breed for you, you must decide on your intentions for the puppy: do you want a Finnish Spitz purely as a pet or are you looking for a potential show dog? If you live in a country where the breed is worked, a future working dog may be your prime interest. Your main reason for wishing to own a Finnish Spitz should be made clear to the breeder when you make your initial inquiries. If you hope to exhibit, you will need to take the breeder's advice as to which available puppy shows the most promise for the show ring. If looking for a pet, you should discuss your family situation with the breeder and take his advice as to which puppy is likely to suit you best.

Before visiting a litter, you should do plenty of "homework" on the breed and suitable breeders. You should visit at least one dog show, either a specialty show for Finnish Spitzen only or an all-breed show where there is an entry of Finnish Spitzen. Such a visit will provide you with a chance to see a number of the breed in action and to watch the dogs interact with their breeders and owners. You will be able to see dogs of different lines and perhaps one line will particularly appeal to you. If you approach the handlers when they are not busy with the dogs, most will be happy to recommend or introduce you to breeders.

The American Kennel Club and the Finnish Spitz Club of America can certainly point you in the right direction when look-

Are you ready for a Finnish addition to the family? Hannah and her Finnish Spitz are the best of friends.

ing for a reputable breeder. Members of breed clubs are required to follow strict codes of ethics in their breeding programs, so you can be assured that these breeders produce puppies with the goal of bettering the breed and that they are not motivated by profit. Contact several breeders, talk to them by phone, visit their premises, etc., even if there is no litter immediately available. It is always important to remember that when looking for a puppy, a good breeder will be assessing you as a prospective new owner just as carefully as you are select-

PUPPY APPEARANCE

Your puppy should have a well-fed appearance but not a distended abdomen, which may indicate worms or incorrect feeding, or both. The body should be firm, with a solid feel. The skin of the abdomen should be pale pink and clean, without signs of scratching or rash. Check the hind legs to see that dewclaws were removed; this is done at a few days old.

ing the breeder. Also keep in mind that many good breeders have waiting lists for their puppies, and Finnish Spitzen do not have large litters to begin with. Three or four puppies in a litter is normal, but there can occasionally be more or fewer. The Finnish Spitz is low in

PEDIGREE VS. REGISTRATION CERTIFICATE

Too often new owners are confused between these two important documents. Your puppy's pedigree, essentially a family tree, is a written record of a dog's genealogy of three generations or more. The pedigree will show you the names as well as performance titles of all dogs in your pup's background. Your breeder must provide you with a registration application, with his part properly filled out. You must complete the application and send it to the AKC with the proper fee. Every puppy must come from a litter that has been AKC-registered by the breeder, born in the US and from a sire and dam that are also registered with the AKC.

The seller must provide you with complete records to identify the puppy. The AKC requires that the seller provide the buyer with the following: breed; sex, color and markings; date of birth; litter number (when available); names and registration numbers of the parents; breeder's name; and date sold or delivered.

number in the US, so your search for a breeder and puppy will take time and will require patience.

Remember when selecting your breeder and your puppy that the dog you select should remain with you for the duration of his life, which will likely be around 13 years, so making the right decision from the outset is of utmost importance. No dog should be moved from one home to another simply because the owners were thoughtless enough not to have done sufficient research and preparation before bringing the puppy home.

You should be confident that your new puppy is healthy and sound, both physically and temperamentally. You should also be comfortable with the breeder, as likely the two of you will be in contact from time to time throughout the dog's life. A breeder is an invaluable resource for a new owner; likewise, breeders often like to keep in touch with owners to make sure that everything is going well.

Breeders commonly allow visitors to see their litters by around the fifth or sixth week, and puppies leave for their new homes between the eighth and tenth week. Breeders who permit their puppies to leave early are more interested in making a profit than in their puppies' well-being. Puppies need to learn the rules of the pack from their dam, and most dams continue teaching the pups manners and dos and don'ts until around the eighth week. Breeders spend significant amounts of time with the Finnish Spitz toddlers so that the pups are able to interact with the "other species," i.e., humans. Given the long history that dogs and humans have, bonding between the two species is natural but must be nurtured. A well-bred, well-socialized Finnish Spitz pup wants nothing more than to be near you and be rewarded.

At your first opportunity to visit a potentially suitable litter, watch the puppies interact together. You will find that different puppies have different personalities, and some will be more boisterous and extroverted than others. It may indeed be tempting

"YOU BETTER SHOP AROUND!"

Finding a reputable breeder who sells healthy pups is very important, but make sure that the breeder you choose is not only someone you respect but also someone with whom you feel comfortable. Your breeder will be a resource long after you buy your puppy, and you must be able to call with reasonable questions without being made to feel like a pest! If you don't connect on a personal level, investigate some other breeders before making a final decision.

to take pity on the unduly shy puppy that sits quietly in a corner, but do bear in mind that this is likely to be a dog that will lack confidence in adulthood. Although you will need to use your own judgment as to which puppy is most likely to fit in with your own lifestyle, you should

Owning a dog is not a "fair-weather" commitment. At the very least, your dog must always be allowed outside to do his business, rain or shine.

also be guided by the breeder's judgment and knowledge.

Puppies almost invariably look enchanting, but you must select one from a caring breeder who has given the puppies all the

TEMPERAMENT COUNTS

Your selection of a good puppy can be determined by your needs. A show potential or a good pet? It is your choice. Every puppy, however, should be of good temperament. Although show-quality puppies are bred and raised with emphasis on physical conformation, responsible breeders strive for equally good temperament. Do not buy from a breeder who concentrates solely on physical beauty at the expense of personality.

attention they deserve and has looked after them well. The puppy you select should look well fed, but not pot-bellied, as this might indicate worms. The eyes should look bright and clear, without discharge. The nose should be moist, an indication of good health, but should never be runny. It goes without saying that there should certainly be no evidence of loose motions or parasites. The puppy you choose should also have a healthy-looking coat, an important indication of good health internally. Always check the bite of your selected puppy to be sure that it is neither overshot nor undershot. This may not be too noticeable on a young puppy, but will become more evident as the puppy gets older.

Do you have a preference for a male or a female puppy? As previously discussed, there are some differences between the genders. Dogs should be easily distinguishable from bitches; they are larger than bitches and carry considerably more coat. Masculinity and femininity should also show clearly in the head. Personality-wise, males can tend to be more dominant.

Something else to consider is whether or not to take out veterinary insurance. Vet's bills can mount up, and you must always be certain that sufficient funds are available to give your dog any veterinary attention that may be needed. Policies available today are very varied, ranging from those that cover emergencies only to those that encompass checkups and other routine care.

COMMITMENT OF OWNERSHIP
After considering all of the factors that go into bringing a puppy into your home, you have most likely already made some very important decisions. You have chosen the Finnish Spitz, which means that you have decided which characteristics you want in a dog and what type of dog will best fit into your family and lifestyle. If you have selected a breeder, you have gone a step further—you have done your research and found a responsible, conscientious person who breeds quality Finnish Spitzen and who should be a reliable source of help as you and your puppy adjust to life together. If you have observed a litter in action, you have obtained a firsthand look at the dynamics

Research your pup's pedigree and background thoroughly. Prize-winning dogs in your pup's recent ancestry gives you assurance of quality breeding.

of a puppy "pack" and, thus, you have learned about each pup's individual personality—perhaps you have even found one that particularly appeals to you.

However, even if you have not yet found the Finnish Spitz puppy of your dreams, observing pups will help you learn to recognize certain behavior and to determine what a pup's behavior indicates about his temperament. You will be able to pick out which pups are the leaders, which ones are less outgoing, which ones are confident, shy, playful, friendly, aggressive, etc. Equally as important, you will learn to recognize what a healthy pup should look and act like. All of these things will help you in your search, and when you find the Finnish Spitz that was meant for you, you will know it!

Researching your breed, selecting a responsible breeder and observing as many pups as

BOY OR GIRL?
An important consideration to be discussed is the sex of your puppy. For a family companion, a bitch may be the better choice, considering the female's inbred concern for all young creatures and her accompanying tolerance and patience. It is always advisable to spay a pet bitch or neuter a pet male, which may guarantee your Finnish Spitz a longer life.

ARE YOU PREPARED?

Unfortunately, when a puppy is bought by someone who does not take into consideration the time and attention that dog ownership requires, it is the puppy who suffers when he is either abandoned or placed in a shelter by a frustrated owner. So all of the "homework" you do in preparation for your pup's arrival will benefit you both. The more informed you are, the more you will know what to expect and the better equipped you will be to handle the ups and downs of raising a puppy. Hopefully, everyone in the household is willing to do his part in raising and caring for the pup. The anticipation of owning a dog often brings a lot of promises from excited family members: "I will walk him every day," "I will feed him," "I will housebreak him," etc., but these things take time and effort, and promises can easily be forgotten once the novelty of the new pet has worn off.

possible are all important steps on the way to dog ownership. It may seem like a lot of effort...and you have not even taken the pup home yet! Remember, though, you cannot be too careful when it comes to deciding on the type of dog you want and finding out about your prospective pup's background. Buying a puppy is not—or *should* not be—just another whimsical purchase. This is one instance in which you actually do get to choose your own family! You may be thinking that buying a puppy should be fun—it should not be so serious and so much work. Keep in mind that your puppy is not a cuddly stuffed toy or decorative lawn ornament; rather, he is a living

creature that will become a real member of your family. You will come to realize that, while buying a puppy is a pleasurable and exciting endeavor, it is not something to be taken lightly. Relax...the fun will start when the pup comes home!

Always keep in mind that a puppy is nothing more than a baby in a furry disguise...a baby who is virtually helpless in a human world and who trusts his owner for fulfillment of his basic needs for survival. In addition to food, water and shelter, your pup needs care, protection, guidance and love. If you are not prepared to commit to this, then you are not prepared to own a dog.

"Wait a minute," you say.

"How hard could this be? All of my neighbors own dogs and they seem to be doing just fine. Why should I have to worry about all of this?" Well, you should not worry about it; in fact, you will probably find that once your Finnish Spitz pup gets used to his new home, he will fall into his place in the family quite naturally. However, it never hurts to emphasize the commitment of dog ownership. With some time and patience, it is really not too difficult to raise a curious and exuberant Finnish Spitz pup to be a well-adjusted and well-mannered adult dog—a dog that could be your most loyal friend.

Dog owners have found that gates designed for use in the home with toddlers are equally effective in securing dogs in their designated areas.

PREPARING PUPPY'S PLACE IN YOUR HOME

Researching your breed and finding a breeder are only two aspects of the homework you will have to do before taking your Finnish Spitz puppy home. You will also have to prepare your home and family for the new addition. Much as you would prepare a nursery for a newborn baby, you will need to designate a place in your home that will be the puppy's own. How you prepare your home will depend on how much freedom the dog will be allowed. Whatever you decide, you must ensure that he has a place that he can "call his own."

When you bring your new puppy into your home, you are bringing him into what will become his home as well. Obviously, you did not buy a puppy with the intentions of catering to his every whim and

THE COCOA WARS

Chocolate contains the chemical thebromine, which is poisonous to dogs, although "chocolates" especially made for dogs are safe (as they don't actually contain chocolate) but not recommended. Any item that encourages your dog to enjoy the taste of cocoa should be discouraged. You should also exercise caution when using mulch in your garden. This frequently contains cocoa hulls, and dogs have been known to die from eating the mulch.

Your local pet shop will have a variety of suitable crates. Obtain a crate for your Finnish Spitz puppy that will comfortably house him at his full size.

PHOTO COURTESY OF DOSKOCIL

take him long to get used to it, but the sudden shock of being transplanted is somewhat traumatic for a young pup. Imagine how a small child would feel in the same situation—that is how your puppy must be feeling. It is up to you to reassure him and to let him know, "Little Finkie, you are going to like it here!"

WHAT YOU SHOULD BUY

CRATE

To someone unfamiliar with the use of crates in dog training, it may seem like punishment to shut a dog in a crate, but this is not the case at all. More and more breeders and trainers around the world are recommending crates as preferred tools for pet puppies as well as show puppies. Crates are not cruel—crates have many humane and highly effective uses in dog care and training. For example, crate-training is a popular and very successful house-breaking method. In addition, a crate can keep your dog safe during travel and, perhaps most importantly, a crate provides your dog with a place of his own in your home. It serves as a "doggie bedroom" of sorts—your Finnish Spitz can curl up in his crate when he wants to sleep or when he just needs a break. Many dogs sleep in their crates overnight. With soft bedding and his favorite toy, a crate becomes a cozy

allowing him to "rule the roost," but in order for a puppy to grow into a stable, well-adjusted dog, he has to feel comfortable in his surroundings. Remember, he is leaving the warmth and security of his mother and littermates, as well as the familiarity of the only place he has ever known, so it is important to make his transition as easy as possible. By preparing a place in your home for the puppy, you are making him feel as welcome as possible in a strange new place. It should not pseudo-den for your dog. Like his ancestors, he too will seek out the comfort and retreat of a den—you just happen to be providing him with something a little more luxurious than what his early ancestors enjoyed.

As far as purchasing a crate, the type that you buy is up to you. It will most likely be one of the two most popular types: wire or fiberglass. There are advantages and disadvantages to each type. For example, a wire crate is more open, allowing the air to flow through and affording the dog a view of what is going on around him, while a fiberglass crate is sturdier. Both can be used for car travel, providing protection for the dog, but an airline-approved fiberglass crate is required for air travel.

The size of the crate is another thing to consider. Puppies do not stay puppies forever—in fact, sometimes it seems as if they grow right before your eyes. A small crate may be fine for a very young Finnish Spitz pup, but it will not do him much good for long! It is better from the outset to obtain a crate that will accommodate your dog both as a pup and at full size. For a Finnish Spitz, a crate of about 26" by 21" by 24" should be suitable for traveling purposes (depending on the size of your Finnish Spitz), but a larger crate is necessary for use inside the home.

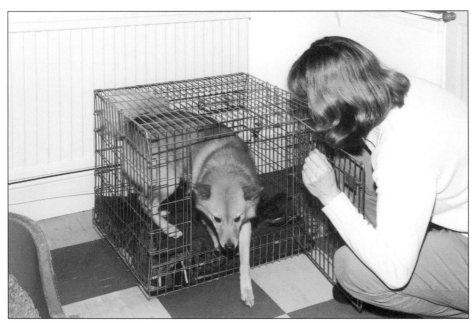

Simply put, there is no better structure for your Finnish Spitz than being crate-trained. When you are at home, the crate door can be left open so the dog can enter and exit as he pleases.

a potty "accident" in his crate, and replace or remove any padding or blanket that becomes ragged and starts to fall apart.

TOYS

Toys are a must for dogs of all ages, especially for curious, playful pups. Puppies are the "children" of the dog world, and what child does not love toys? Chew toys provide enjoyment for both dog and owner—your dog will enjoy playing with his favorite toys, while you will enjoy the fact that they distract him from chewing on your expensive shoes and leather sofa. Puppies love to chew; in fact, chewing is a physical need for pups as they are teething, and everything looks appetizing! The full range of your possessions—from old slippers to Oriental carpet—are fair game in the eyes of a teething pup. Puppies are not all that discerning when it comes to finding something literally to "sink their teeth into"—everything tastes great!

The Finnish Spitz is not normally known as a particularly aggressive chewer, but will enjoy toys. Any toys offered should be completely safe and made specifically for dogs, with no removable parts. Hard nylon bones and chews are good choices, as they are very durable and will not break into small pieces.

Many dogs enjoy playing with squeaky toys, but these should

In addition to his crate, your puppy will appreciate a cozy dog bed in which he can cuddle up.

BEDDING

A soft crate pad and a cuddly blanket inside the dog's crate will help the dog feel more at home. First, these items will take the place of the leaves, twigs, etc., that the pup would use in the wild to make a den; the pup can make his own "burrow" in the crate. Although your pup is far removed from his den-making ancestors, the denning instinct is still a part of his genetic makeup. Second, until you take your pup home, he has been sleeping amid the warmth of his mother and littermates, and while a blanket is not the same as a warm, breathing body, it still provides heat and something with which to snuggle. You will want to wash your pup's bedding frequently in case he has always be checked regularly to see that there is no danger of the "squeaker" mechanism's becoming loose and being swallowed. Likewise, breeders advise owners to resist stuffed toys, because they can become de-stuffed in no time. The overly excited pup may ingest the stuffing, which is neither nutritious nor digestible.

Monitor the condition of all of your pup's toys carefully and get rid of any that have been chewed to the point of becoming potentially dangerous. Be careful of natural bones, which have a tendency to splinter into sharp, dangerous pieces. Also be careful of rawhide, which can turn into pieces that are easy to swallow and become a mushy mess on your carpet.

LEASH

A nylon leash is probably the best option, as it is the most resistant to puppy teeth should your pup take a liking to chewing on his leash. Of course, this is a habit that should be nipped in the bud, but, if your pup likes to chew on his leash, he has a very slim chance of being able to chew through the strong nylon. Nylon leashes are also lightweight, which is good for a young Finnish Spitz who is just getting used to the idea of walking on a leash. For everyday walking and safety purposes, the nylon leash is a good choice. As your pup grows

up and gets used to walking on the leash, you may want to purchase a flexible leash. These leashes allow you to extend the length to give the dog a broader area to explore or to shorten the length to keep the dog near you.

TOYS, TOYS, TOYS!

With a big variety of dog toys available, and so many that look like they would be a lot of fun for a dog, be careful in your selection. It is amazing what a set of dog teeth can do to an innocent-looking toy, so, obviously, safety is a major consideration. Be sure to choose the most durable products that you can find. Hard nylon bones and toys are a safe bet, and many of them are offered in different scents and flavors that will be sure to capture your dog's attention. It is always fun to play a game of fetch with your dog, and there are balls and flying discs that are specially made to withstand dog teeth.

There is a wide range of leashes available from which you may choose one suitable for your Finnish Spitz.

COLLAR

Your pup should get used to wearing a collar all the time since you will want to attach his ID tags to it; plus, you have to attach the leash to something! A lightweight nylon collar is a good choice. Make certain that the collar fits snugly enough so that the pup cannot wriggle out of it, but is loose enough so that it will not be uncomfortably tight around the pup's neck. You should be able to fit a finger between the pup's neck and the collar. It may take some time for your pup to get used to wearing the collar, but soon he will not even notice that it is there.

Choke collars are made for training, but are not recommended for use on heavily coated breeds. The abundant ruff around the Finnish Spitz's neck makes a chain choke collar inappropriate for this breed, as the coat can easily be pulled and damaged by this type of collar.

FOOD AND WATER BOWLS

Your pup will need two bowls, one for food and one for water. You may want two sets of bowls, one for indoors and one for outdoors, depending on where the dog will be fed and where he will be spending time. Stainless steel or sturdy plastic bowls are popular choices. Plastic bowls are more chewable, but dogs tend not to chew on the steel variety, which can be sterilized. It is important to buy sturdy bowls since anything is in danger of being chewed by puppy teeth and you do not want your dog to be constantly chewing apart his bowl (for his safety and for your wallet!).

CLEANING SUPPLIES

Until a pup is housebroken, you will be doing a lot of cleaning. "Accidents" will occur, which is acceptable in the beginning stages of toilet training because the puppy does not know any better. All you can do is be prepared to clean up any accidents as soon as they happen. Old rags, paper towels, newspapers and a safe disinfectant are good to have on hand.

CHOOSE AN APPROPRIATE COLLAR

The **BUCKLE COLLAR** is the standard collar used for everyday purposes. Be sure that you adjust the buckle on growing puppies. Check it every day. It can become too tight overnight! These collars can be made of leather or nylon. Attach your dog's identification tags to this collar.

The **CHOKE COLLAR** is designed for use during training. It is constructed of highly polished steel so that it slides easily through the stainless steel loop. The idea is that the dog controls the pressure around his neck and he will stop pulling if the collar becomes uncomfortable. It is *not* suitable for use with the heavily coated Finnish Spitz.

The **HALTER** is for a trained dog that has to be restrained to prevent running away, chasing a cat and the like. Considered the most humane of all collars, it is frequently used on smaller dogs on which collars are not comfortable.

Choose durable, easily cleaned food and water bowls of appropriate size for your Finnish Spitz.

BEYOND THE BASICS

The items previously discussed are the bare necessities. You will find out what else you need as you go along—grooming supplies, flea/tick protection, baby gates to partition a room, etc. These things will vary depending on your situation, but it is important that you have everything you need to feed and make your Finnish Spitz comfortable in his first few days at home.

PUPPY-PROOFING YOUR HOME

Aside from making sure that your Finnish Spitz will be comfortable in your home, you also have to make sure that your home is safe for your Finnish Spitz. This means taking precautions that your pup will not get into anything he should not get into and that there is nothing within his reach that may harm him should he sniff it, chew it, inspect it, etc. This probably seems obvious since, while you are primarily concerned with your pup's safety, at the same time you do not want your belongings to be ruined. Breakables should be placed out of reach if your dog is to have full run of the house. If he is to be limited to certain places within the house, keep any potentially dangerous items in the "off-limits" areas.

An electrical cord can pose a danger should the puppy decide to taste it—and who is going to convince a pup that it would not make a great chew toy? All cords and wires should be fastened tightly against the wall, out of the puppy's sight and away from his teeth. If your dog is going to spend time in a crate, make sure that there is nothing near his crate that he can reach if he sticks his curious little paws through the openings. Just as you would with a child, keep all household cleaners and chemicals where the pup cannot reach them.

It is just as important to make sure that the outside of your home is safe. Of course, your puppy should never be unsupervised, but a pup let loose in the yard will want to run and explore, and he should be granted that freedom. Do not let a fence give you a false sense of security; you would be surprised at how crafty (and persistent) a dog can be in figuring out how to dig under a fence and squeeze his way through small holes, or to jump or climb over a fence. The remedy is to make the fence well embedded into the ground and high enough so that it really is impossible for your dog to get over it. A four-foot fence should be sufficient, but an even higher fence would be prudent if your Finnish Spitz is talented in the art of escape, as some can be. It is best to err on the side of caution.

Be sure to repair or secure any gaps in the fence. Check the fence

It is your responsibility to clean up after your dog has relieved himself. Pet shops have various aids to assist in the cleanup job.

periodically to ensure that it remains in good shape; a very determined pup may return to the same spot to "work on it" until he is able to get through.

FIRST TRIP TO THE VET

You have selected your puppy, and your home and family are ready. Now all you have to do is collect your Finnish Spitz from the breeder and the fun begins, right? Well...not so fast. Something else you need to plan is your pup's first trip to the veterinarian. Perhaps the breeder can recommend someone in the area who has experience with the

NATURAL TOXINS

Examine your grass and landscaping before bringing your puppy home. Many varieties of plants have leaves, stems or flowers that are toxic if ingested, and you can depend on a curious puppy to investigate them. Ask your vet for information on poisonous plants or research them at your library.

If you see your dog carrying a piece of vegetation in his mouth, approach him in a quiet, disinterested manner, avoid eye contact, pet him and gradually remove the plant from his mouth. Alternatively, offer him a treat and maybe he'll drop the plant on his own. Be sure no toxic plants are growing in your yard or kept in your home.

Finnish Spitz or other spitz breeds, or maybe you know some dog owners who can suggest a good vet. Either way, you should have an appointment arranged for your pup before you pick him up.

The pup's first visit will consist of an overall examination to make sure that the pup does not have any problems that are not apparent to you. The vet will also set up a schedule for the pup's vaccinations; the breeder will inform you of which ones the pup has already received and the vet can continue from there.

INTRODUCTION TO THE FAMILY

Everyone in the house will be excited about the puppy's coming home and will want to pet him and play with him, but it is best to make the introductions low-key so as not to overwhelm the puppy. He is apprehensive already. It is the first time he has been separated from his mother and the breeder, and the ride to your home is likely to be the first time he has been in a car. The last thing you want to do is smother him, as this will only frighten him further. This is not to say that human contact is not extremely necessary at this stage, because this is the time when a connection between the pup and his human family is formed. Gentle petting and soothing words should help console him, as well as just putting the pup down and letting him explore on his own (under your watchful eye, of course).

The pup may approach the family members or may busy himself with exploring for a while. Gradually, each person should spend some time with the pup, one at a time, crouching down to get as close to the pup's level as possible, letting him sniff each person's hands and petting him gently. He definitely needs human attention and he needs to be touched—this is how to form an immediate bond. Just remember that the pup is experiencing many things for the first time, at the same time. There are new people, new noises, new smells and new things to investigate, so be gentle, be affectionate and be as comforting as you can be.

PUP'S FIRST NIGHT HOME

You have traveled home with your new charge safely in his crate. He's been to the vet for a thorough check-up; he's been weighed, his papers have been examined and perhaps he's even been vaccinated and wormed as well. He's met (and licked!) the whole family, including the excited children and the less-than-happy cat. He's explored his area, his new bed, the yard and anywhere else he's been permitted. He's eaten his first meal at home and relieved himself in the proper place. He's heard lots of

new sounds, smelled new friends and seen more of the outside world than ever before…and that was just the first day! He's worn out and is ready for bed…or so you think!

It's puppy's first night home and you are ready to say "Good night." Keep in mind that this is his first night ever to be sleeping alone. His dam and littermates are no longer at paw's length and he's a bit scared, cold and lonely. Be reassuring to your new family member, but this is not the time to spoil him and give in to his inevitable whining.

Puppies whine. They whine to let others know where they are and hopefully to get company out of it. Place your pup in his new bed or crate in his designated area and close the crate door. Mercifully, he may fall asleep without a peep. When the inevitable occurs, however, ignore

Six-week-old littermates. Until your Finnish Spitz pup comes home with you, he has had the constant companionship of his siblings. Being separated from them is a big change for a young pup, so be comforting and help him settle in when he first comes home.

the whining—he is fine. Be strong and keep his interest in mind. Do not allow yourself to feel guilty and visit the pup. He will fall asleep eventually.

Many breeders recommend placing a piece of bedding from the pup's former home in his new bed so that he recognizes and is comforted by the scent of his littermates. Others still advise placing a hot water bottle in the bed for warmth. The latter may be a good idea, provided the pup doesn't attempt to suckle—he'll get good and wet, and may not fall asleep so fast.

Puppy's first night can be somewhat stressful for both the pup and his new family. Remember that you are setting the tone of nighttime at your house. Unless you want to play with your pup every night at 10 p.m., midnight and 2 a.m., don't initiate the habit. Your family will thank you, and eventually so will your puppy!

PREVENTING PUPPY PROBLEMS

SOCIALIZATION

Now that you have done all of the preparatory work and have helped your pup get accustomed to his new home and family, it is about time for you to have some fun! Socializing your Finnish Spitz pup gives you the opportunity to show off your new friend, and

PET INSURANCE

Just like you can insure your car, your house and your own health, you likewise can insure your dog's health. Investigate a pet insurance policy by talking to your vet. Depending on the age of your dog, the breed and the kind of coverage you desire, your policy can be very affordable. Most policies cover accidental injuries, poisoning and thousands of medical problems and illnesses, including cancers. Some carriers also offer routine care and immunization coverage.

your pup gets to reap the benefits of being an adorable furry creature that people will want to pet and, in general, think is absolutely precious!

Besides getting to know his new family, your puppy should be exposed to other people, animals and situations. This will help him become well adjusted as he grows up and less prone to being timid or fearful of the new things he will encounter. Of course, he must not come into close contact with dogs you don't know well until his course of injections is fully complete.

Your pup's socialization began with the breeder, but now it is your responsibility to continue it. The socialization he receives until the age of 12 weeks is the most critical, as this is the time when he forms his impressions of the outside world. Be especially careful during the eight-to-ten-week-old period, also known as the fear period. The interaction that the pup receives during this time should be gentle and reassuring. Lack of socialization, and/or negative experiences during the socialization period, can manifest itself in fear and aggression as the dog grows up. Your puppy needs lots of positive interaction, which of course includes human contact, affection, handling and exposure to other animals.

Once your pup has received his necessary vaccinations, feel free to take him out and about (on his leash, of course). Walk him around the neighborhood, take him on your daily errands, let people pet him, let him meet other dogs and pets, etc. Puppies do not have to try to make friends; there will be no shortage of people who will want to introduce themselves, and many

DANGER!
Scour your garage for potential puppy dangers. Remove weed killers, pesticides and antifreeze materials. Antifreeze is highly toxic and just a few drops can kill a puppy or an adult dog. The sweet taste attracts the animal, who will quickly consume it from the floor or pavement. Also be cautious of items and tools in the garage and left outdoors, because everything looks interesting to a pup and invites his exploration. Don't let your pup follow his nose into danger.

people you will meet will be intrigued by your enchanting red spitz. Just make sure that you carefully supervise each meeting. If the neighborhood children want to say hello, for example, that is great—children and pups most often make great companions. However, sometimes an excited child can unintentionally handle a pup too roughly, or an overzealous pup can playfully nip a little too hard. You want to make socialization experiences positive ones. What a pup learns during this very formative stage will affect his attitude toward future encounters. You want your dog to

Finnish Spitz and children are natural friends if properly introduced. This dog enjoys the company of his best buddy Sam.

PROPER SOCIALIZATION
The socialization period for puppies is from age 8 to 16 weeks. This is the time when puppies need to leave their birth family and take up residence with their new owners, where they will meet many new people and other pets, experience new things, etc. Failure to be adequately socialized can cause the dog to grow up fearing others and being shy and unfriendly due to a lack of self-confidence.

---

be comfortable around everyone. A pup that has a bad experience with a child may grow up to be a dog that is shy around or aggressive toward children.

CONSISTENCY IN TRAINING
Dogs, being pack animals, naturally need a leader, or else they try to establish dominance in their packs. When you welcome a dog into your family, the choice of who becomes the leader and who becomes the pack is entirely up to you! Your pup's intuitive quest for dominance, coupled with the fact that it is nearly impossible to look at an adorable Finnish Spitz pup with his sparkling "puppy-dog" eyes and not cave in, give the pup an almost unfair advantage in getting the upper hand!

A pup will definitely test the waters to see what he can and cannot do. Do not give in to those pleading eyes—stand your ground when it comes to disciplining the pup and make sure that all family members do the same. It will only confuse the pup if Mother tells him to get off the sofa when he is used to sitting up there with Father to watch the nightly news. Avoid discrepancies by having all members of the household decide on the rules before the pup even comes home...and be consistent in enforcing them! Early training shapes the dog's personality, so you cannot be unclear in what you expect.

COMMON PUPPY PROBLEMS

The best way to prevent puppy problems is to be proactive in stopping an undesirable behavior as soon as it starts. The old saying "You can't teach an old dog new tricks" does not necessarily hold

MANNERS MATTER

During the socialization process, a puppy should meet people, experience different environments and definitely be exposed to other canines. Through playing and interacting with other dogs, your puppy will learn lessons, ranging from controlling the pressure of his jaws by biting his littermates to the inner-workings of the canine pack that he will apply to his human relationships for the rest of his life. That is why removing a puppy from the litter too early (before eight weeks) can be detrimental to the pup's development.

true, but it *is* true that it is much easier to discourage bad behavior in a young developing pup than to wait until the pup's bad behavior becomes the adult dog's bad habit. There are some problems that are especially prevalent in puppies as they develop.

NIPPING

As puppies start to teethe, they feel the need to sink their teeth into anything that's available... unfortunately, that usually includes your fingers, arms, hair and toes. You may find this behavior cute for the first five seconds...until you feel just how sharp those puppy teeth are. Nipping is something you want to discourage immediately and consistently with a firm "No!" (or whatever number of firm "Nos" it takes for him to understand that

The more to which a dog is exposed, the more stable he will be in new situations. These lucky Finnish Spitzen have the opportunity to socialize daily with their equine pals.

STRESS-FREE
Some experts in canine health advise that stress during a dog's early years of development can compromise and weaken his immune system, and may trigger the potential for a shortened life. They emphasize the need for happy and stress-free growing-up years.

you mean business). Then, replace your finger with an appropriate chew toy. While this behavior is merely annoying when the dog is young, it can become dangerous as your Finnish Spitz's adult teeth grow in and his jaws develop if he continues to think it is okay to nibble on people. Your Finnish Spitz does not mean any harm with a friendly nip, but he also does not know that his friendly nip is hurting his friend!

CRYING/WHINING

Your pup will often cry, whine, whimper, howl or make some type of commotion when he is left alone. This is basically his way of calling out for attention to make sure that you know he is there and that you have not forgotten about him. Your puppy feels insecure when he is left alone, when you are out of the house and he is in his crate or when you are in another part of the house and he cannot see you. The noise he is making is an expression of the

anxiety he feels at being alone, so he needs to be taught that being alone is okay. You are not actually training the dog to stop making noise; rather, you are training him to feel comfortable when he is alone and thus removing the need for him to make the noise.

This is where the crate with cozy bedding and a toy comes in handy. You want to know that your pup is safe when you are not there to supervise, and you know that he will be safe in his crate rather than roaming freely about the house. In order for the pup to stay in his crate without making a fuss, he first needs to be comfortable in his crate. On that note, it is extremely important that the crate is never used as a form of punishment; this will cause the pup to view the crate as a negative place, rather than as a place of his own for safety and retreat.

Accustom the pup to the crate in short, gradually increasing time intervals in which you put him in the crate, maybe with a treat, and stay in the room with him. If he cries or makes a fuss, do not go to him, but stay in his sight. Gradually the puppy will realize that staying in his crate is fine without your help, and it will not be so traumatic for him when you are not around. You may want to leave the radio on softly when you leave the house; the sound of human voices may be comforting to him.

All puppies of all breeds need to chew. They seem particularly attracted to items that bear their owner's familiar scent. This ardent chewer certainly doesn't mind that the shoe is still on his master's foot!

Finnish Spitzen can be very enthusiastic about "people-food" snacks, but it's best to ignore your dog's pleas. By not giving in to a beggar, you are encouraging proper behavior and keeping his health in mind.

FEEDING CONSIDERATIONS

A Finnish Spitz should be fed sensibly on a high-quality diet, but with so many first-rate canine food products now available, it will be very much a matter of personal preference as to which one is chosen. When purchasing a puppy, a carefully selected breeder should be able to give good advice about feeding your Finnish Spitz throughout his life, including recommendations on types of food. Remember that commercial complete diets should contain all of the nutrients that your dog needs, so supplementing the food should not be necessary unless under special circumstances as advised by your vet.

When you buy your puppy, the breeder should provide you

with a diet sheet that gives details of exactly how your puppy has been fed. Of course you will be at liberty to change that food, together with the frequency and timing of meals, as the youngster reaches adulthood, but this should be done gradually. It is never wise to change suddenly from one diet to another, for this is likely to result in an upset stomach.

The Finnish Spitz does not require a great deal of food, for the breed utilizes its food intake very efficiently. However, most Finnish Spitzen thoroughly enjoy eating, so it is not difficult for

Whether you choose to feed a packaged dog food or prepare your own fresh-food diet, optimal nutrition in the right balance is the prime concern. Your dog's proper diet will be revealed in his well-conditioned body and luminous coat.

TEST FOR PROPER DIET

A good test for proper diet is the color, odor and firmness of your dog's stool. A healthy dog usually produces three semi-hard stools per day. The stools should have no unpleasant odor. They should be the same color from excretion to excretion.

FOOD PREFERENCE

Selecting the best dry dog food is difficult. There is no majority consensus among veterinary scientists as to the value of nutrient analysis (protein, fat, fiber, moisture, ash, cholesterol, minerals, etc.). All agree that feeding trials are what matter most, but you also have to consider the individual dog. The dog's weight, age and activity level, and what pleases his taste, all must be considered. It is probably best to take the advice of your veterinarian. Every dog has individual dietary requirements, and should be fed accordingly.

If your dog is fed a good dry food, he does not require supplements of meat or vegetables. Dogs do appreciate a little variety in their diets, so you may choose to stay with the same brand but vary the flavor. Alternatively, you may wish to add a little flavored stock to give a difference to the taste.

them to put on excess weight. Obesity is as much of a health risk in dogs as it is in humans and contributes to the likelihood of the dog's developing health problems. Feeding any dog too many treats in between meals will increase the risk of the dog's becoming unhealthy and overweight. It is therefore important to keep treats given to a Finnish Spitz to a minimum, and any treats offered should be low in fat. Carrots are excellent treats for a dog, for they will not cause the dog to gain weight and have the additional benefit of helping to keep the dog's teeth clean.

Some owners like to feed fresh food rather than commercial diets. In this case, the responsibility falls on the owner to create a nutritionally complete and balanced diet. It is also worth bearing in mind that if your Finnish Spitz is a "finicky eater," although you have to be very careful not to unbalance an otherwise balanced complete meal, sometimes a little added fresh meat, or even just gravy or stock, will gain a dog's interest and stimulate his appetite.

TYPES OF FOOD

Today the choices of food for your dog are many and varied. You will find dozens of brands of food in all sorts of flavors and textures, ranging from puppy diets to those for senior dogs. There are even

FEEDING TIPS

- Dog food must be served at room temperature, neither too hot nor too cold. Fresh water, changed often and served in a clean bowl, is mandatory, especially when feeding dry food.
- Never feed your dog from the table while you are eating, and never feed your dog leftovers from your own meal. They usually contain too much fat and too much seasoning.
- Dogs must chew their food. Hard pellets are excellent; soups and stews are to be avoided.
- Don't add leftovers or any extras to commercial dog food. The normal food is usually balanced, and adding something extra destroys the balance.
- Except for age-related changes, dogs do not require dietary variations. They can be fed the same diet, day after day, without their becoming bored or ill.

hypoallergenic and low-calorie diets available. Because your Finnish Spitz's food has a bearing on coat, health and temperament, it is essential that the most suitable diet is selected for a dog of his age. It is fair to say, however, that even experienced owners can be perplexed by the enormous range of foods available. Only understanding what is best for your dog will help you reach an informed decision.

Dog foods are produced in three basic types: dry, semi-moist and canned. Dry foods are useful for the cost-conscious, for overall they tend to be less expensive than semi-moist or canned foods. Dry foods also contain the least fat and the most preservatives. In general, canned foods are made up of 60–70% water, while semi-moist ones often contain so much sugar that they are perhaps the least preferred by owners, even though their dogs seem to like them. When selecting your dog's diet, three stages of development must be considered: the puppy stage, the adult stage and the senior stage.

PUPPY STAGE

Puppies instinctively want to suck milk from their mother's teats; a normal puppy will exhibit this behavior just a few moments following birth. If puppies do not attempt to suckle within the first half-hour or so, the breeder should encourage them to do so by placing

A hungry litter gathers 'round the food bowl. Soft solid foods are introduced to the pups as a part of the weaning process.

A Worthy Investment

**Veterinary studies have proven that a balanced high-quality diet
pays off in your dog's coat quality, behavior and activity level.
Invest in premium brands for the maximum payoff with your dog.**

There is no better nutrition for puppies during the first weeks of life than their mother's milk.

them on the nipples, having selected ones with plenty of milk. This early milk supply is important in providing the essential colostrum, which protects the puppies during the first eight to ten weeks of their lives. Although a mother's milk is much better than any commercially prepared milk formula, despite there being some excellent ones available, if the puppies do not feed, the breeder will have to feed them by hand. For those with less experi-ence, advice from a vet is important so that not only the right quantity of milk is fed but also that of correct quality, fed at suit-ably frequent intervals, usually every two hours during the first few days of life.

Puppies should be allowed to nurse from their mother for about the first six weeks, although, start-ing around the third or fourth week, the breeder will begin to introduce small portions of suit-able solid food. Most breeders like to introduce alternate milk and meat meals initially, building up to weaning time.

By the time the puppies are seven or a maximum of eight weeks old, they should be fully weaned and fed solely on a proprietary puppy food. Selection of the most suitable, good-quality diet at this time is essential, for a puppy's fastest growth rate is during the first year of life. Your vet and breeder should be able to offer advice in this regard.

As the puppy grows, the frequency of meals will be reduced over time, and eventually the pup will be switched to an adult diet. Puppy and junior diets should be well balanced for the needs of your dog so that, except in certain circumstances, additional vitamins, minerals and proteins will not be required.

ADULT DIETS

A Finnish Spitz is considered to have reached full adult development at about three-and-a-half to four years old; this is a slow-maturing breed. However, the Finnish Spitz will reach full height well before this time. In general, the diet of a Finnish Spitz can be changed to an adult one at about 10 to 12 months of age, depending on the individual dog's bodily development and the type of food used. Again you should rely upon your vet or breeder to recommend an acceptable mainte-

nance diet. Major dog-food manufacturers specialize in this type of food, and it is merely necessary for you to select the one best suited to your dog's needs. Active dogs may have different requirements than more sedate dogs.

SENIOR DIETS

As dogs get older, their metabolism changes. The older dog usually exercises less, moves more slowly and sleeps more. This change in lifestyle and physiological performance requires a change

---

"DOES THIS COLLAR MAKE ME LOOK FAT?"
While humans may obsess about how they look and how trim their bodies are, many people believe that extra weight on their dogs is a good thing. The truth is, pets should not be over- or under-weight, as both can lead to or signal sickness. In order to tell how fit your pet is, run your hands over his ribs. Are his ribs buried under a layer of fat or are they sticking out considerably? If your pet is within his normal weight range, you should be able to feel the ribs easily, but they should not protrude abnormally. If you stand above him, the outline of his body should resemble an hourglass. Some breeds do tend to be leaner while some are a bit stockier, but making sure your dog is the right weight for his breed will certainly contribute to his good health.

in diet. Since these changes take place slowly, they might not be recognizable. What is easily recognizable is weight gain. By continuing to feed your dog an adult-maintenance diet when he is slowing down metabolically, your dog will gain weight. Obesity in an older dog compounds the health problems that already

Diet plays a big role in the older dog's health, vitality and overall condition. This is a sprightly-looking, alert 11-year-old.

THE CANINE GOURMET
Your dog does not prefer a fresh bone. Indeed, he wants it properly aged and, if given such a treat indoors, he is more likely to try to bury it in the carpet than he is to settle in for a good chew! If you have a yard, give him such delicacies outside and guide him to a place suitable for his "bone yard." He will carefully place the treasure in its earthy vault and seemingly forget about it. Trust me, his seeming distaste or lack of thanks for your thoughtfulness is not that at all. He will return in a few days to inspect the bone, perhaps to re-bury it, and when it is just right, he will relish it as much as you do that cooked-to-perfection steak. If he is in a concrete or bricked kennel run, he will be especially frustrated at the hopelessness of the situation. He will vacillate between ignoring it completely, giving it a few licks to speed the curing process with saliva, and trying to hide it behind the water bowl! When the bone has aged a bit, he will set to work on it.

accompany old age.

As your dog gets older, few of his organs function up to par. The kidneys slow down and the intestines become less efficient. These age-related factors are best handled with a change in diet and a change in feeding schedule to give smaller portions that are more easily digested. There is no single best diet for every older dog. Some Finnish Spitzen are switched to a senior diet around seven or eight years of age, while others are not. Many dogs do well on light or senior diets, while other dogs do better on puppy diets or special premium diets such as lamb and rice. Be sensitive to your aging Finnish Spitz's diet, as this will help control other problems that may arise with your old friend.

WATER

Just as your dog needs proper nutrition from his food, water is an essential "nutrient" as well. Water keeps the dog's body properly hydrated and promotes normal function of the body's systems. Your Finnish Spitz should have free access to clean fresh water at all times, especially if you feed dry food. Make certain that the dog's water bowl is clean, and change the water often.

Of course, during housebreaking, it is necessary to keep an eye on when and how much water your Finnish Spitz is drinking so that you will be better able to predict when he will need to relieve himself.

EXERCISE

Although the Finnish Spitz is not a very large breed, it is a very active one. Thus, daily exercise is necessary for the breed's health and happiness. A sedentary lifestyle is as harmful to a dog as it is to a person. The Finnish Spitz needs regular activity to stay fit and to expend his considerable energy. A Finnish Spitz that does not get enough exercise will be more prone to obesity and to resorting to destructive behavior due to boredom.

Although the Finnish Spitz is an energetic, active breed that enjoys exercise, you don't have to be an Olympic athlete to provide your dog with a sufficient amount of activity! Exercising your Finnish Spitz can be enjoyable and healthy for both of you. Brisk walks, once the puppy reaches three or four months of age, will stimulate heart rates and build muscle for both dog and owner. As the dog reaches adulthood, the speed and distance of the walks can be increased as long as they are both kept reasonable and comfortable for both of you. Play sessions in your fenced yard and letting the dog run free in a safely enclosed area under your supervision also are sufficient forms of exercise for the Finnish Spitz.

Fetching games can be played indoors or out; these are excellent for giving your dog active play that he will enjoy. Chasing things that move comes naturally to dogs of all breeds, and especially to breeds like the Finnish Spitz that have strong hunting instincts. When your Finnish Spitz runs after the ball or object, praise him for picking it up and encourage him to bring it back to you for another throw. Never go to the object and pick it up yourself, or you'll soon find that you are the one retrieving the objects rather than your dog! If you choose to play games outdoors, you must have a securely fenced-in yard and/or have the dog attached to at least a 25-foot-long light line for security. You want your Finnish Spitz to run, but not run away!

Likewise, when allowing a

dog to run free, whether in your own backyard or a public place like a dog run or park, safety is of the utmost importance. For this reason, you should investigate and secure all possible escape routes before letting your dog off his leash. Never forget that the Finnish Spitz is a hunter, so he might well decide to take you by surprise and run off to chase something that has caught his attention.

Bear in mind that an overweight dog should never be suddenly over-exercised; instead, he should be encouraged to increase exercise slowly. And again, not only is exercise essential to keep the dog's body fit, it is essential to his mental well-being. A bored dog will find something to do, which often manifests itself in some type of behavior that will be unacceptable to the owner. In this sense, the dog's exercise is essential for the owner's mental well-being, too!

GROOMING

ROUTINE COAT MAINTENANCE
The Finnish Spitz is a meticulously clean dog that likes to clean himself frequently. This is not a breed that carries a particularly "doggy" odor. Actually, the Finnish Spitz is often likened to a cat because it is said to have feline qualities, one of which is the love of self-cleaning.

DRINK, DRANK, DRUNK—MAKE IT A DOUBLE
In both humans and dogs, as well as other living organisms, water forms the major part of nearly every body tissue. Naturally, we take water for granted, but without it, life as we know it would cease.

For dogs, water is needed to keep their bodies functioning biochemically. Additionally, water is needed to replace the water lost while panting. Unlike humans, who are able to sweat to dissipate heat, dogs must pant to cool down, thereby losing the vital water that their bodies need to regulate their body temperatures. Humans lose electrolyte-containing products and other body-fluid components through sweating; dogs do not lose anything except water.

Water is essential always, but especially so when the weather is hot or humid or when your dog is exercising or working vigorously.

Your Finnish Spitz will need to have a good brushing on a weekly basis, especially when shedding. The ruff, tail and "pants" will also need to be carefully combed through. It is therefore essential that short grooming sessions be introduced from a very early age. From the very beginning, a few minutes each day should be set aside so that your puppy becomes familiar with the process. Set aside a grooming area, ideally a grooming table with a non-slip surface. This way, your puppy will learn to associate the designated area with his grooming sessions and, of course, to behave. If your puppy is taught to behave well during grooming, it will be a pleasure both for the dog and for you.

Heavy shedding occurs in both dogs and bitches. During times of shedding, combing through the coat on a daily basis will help to keep your home free from shed hairs. However, most of the time, the hairs that fall from the dog to land on your furniture and carpets can easily be picked up with a vacuum.

Different breeders use different methods of grooming and you, too, will eventually find the particular method that suits you and your Finnish Spitz best. Most owners prefer only to bathe their dogs occasionally, so as to preserve the quality of the coat.

Trimming the Finnish Spitz is not to be done. This is a natural breed and must not be sculpted in any way. It is even stated in the breed standard that no trimming is allowed except for the feet. A little trimming under the pads of the feet is sensible to avoid the formation of knots between the toes.

BATHING

Finnish Spitzen need bathing only rarely, as bathing too often removes the natural oils of their skin and coat. Therefore, only bathe your Finnish Spitz when neccessary. Dry-bath products also are an option for the Finnish Spitz. When the need arises, you will want your dog to be at ease in the bath or else it could end up a wet, soapy, messy ordeal for both of you! Therefore, it is wise to give your Finnish Spitz his first

The tail is an important feature of the Finnish Spitz that must be paid special attention. The hair on the curved tail is brushed forward over the back.

bath as a puppy so that he'll be more tolerant of it as an adult.

Brush your Finnish Spitz thoroughly before wetting his coat. This will get rid of most mats, tangles and dead hair, which are harder to remove when the coat is wet. Make certain that your dog has a good non-slip surface on which to stand. Begin by wetting the dog's coat, checking the water temperature to make sure that it is neither too hot nor too cold for the dog. A shower or hose attachment is necessary for thoroughly wetting and rinsing the coat.

Next, apply shampoo to the dog's coat and work it into a good lather. Wash the head last, as you do not want shampoo to drip into the dog's eyes while you are washing the rest of his body. You should use only a shampoo that is made for dogs. Do not use a product made for human hair. Work the shampoo all the way down to the skin. You can use this opportunity to check the skin for any bumps, bites or other abnormalities. Do not neglect any area of the body—get all of the hard-to-reach places.

Once the dog has been thoroughly shampooed, he requires an equally thorough rinsing. Shampoo left in the coat can be drying and irritating to the dog's skin and coat. Protect his eyes from the shampoo by shielding them with your hand and direct-

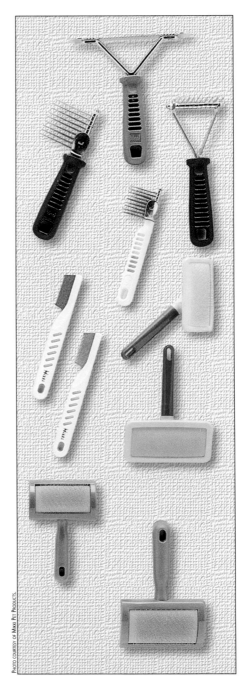

Your pet shop should have all of the necessary grooming tools for maintaining your Finnish Spitz's double coat in top condition.

A double-sided brush is a convenient grooming tool. Here, the shorter hair on the head is brushed with the bristle-brush side.

Using the pin-brush side on the neck area, where the coat is more dense.

ing the flow of water in the opposite direction. You also should avoid getting water in the ear canals.

Once he is rinsed, be prepared for your dog to shake out his coat—you might want to stand back, but make sure you have a hold on the dog to keep him from running through the house. Lift him out of the tub with a heavy towel to soak up some of the moisture. After a good towel-drying, keep your Finnish Spitz indoors until his coat is completely dry; this is especially important in cold weather.

EAR CLEANING

Your Finnish Spitz's ears should be checked weekly for any build-up of dirt and should be cleaned accordingly. Clean the ears with a cotton ball or soft wipe and an ear-cleaning liquid or powder made especially for dogs. Do not probe into the ear canal with a cotton swab or anything else, as this can cause injury.

Be on the lookout for any signs of ear mites; a telltale sign is the presence of dark droppings in the ears. Also, if your dog has been scratching at his ears frequently, this usually indicates a problem. If the dog's ears have an unusual odor, this is a sure sign of mite infestation or infection, and a signal to have his ears checked by the vet.

NAIL CLIPPING

Your Finnish Spitz's nails must also be checked regularly to ensure that they are of an appropriate length, though how much they grow will depend very much on whether your Finnish Spitz exercises on hard surfaces or primarily on grass. Regular walks on pavement or cement surfaces will wear down the nails naturally. In any event, it is important that the nails are checked regularly, because a dog's long nails can scratch someone unintentionally and also have a better chance of ripping, bleeding or causing the feet to spread. A good rule of thumb is that if you can hear your dog's nails' clicking on the floor when he walks, his nails are too long.

It will be helpful for you to accustom your Finnish Spitz to having his nails clipped as a puppy, because some dogs do not like having their feet handled and will not tolerate the procedure as adults if not used to it. Before you start cutting, make sure you can identify the "quick" in each nail. The quick is a blood vessel that runs through the center of each nail and grows rather close to the end. The quick will bleed if accidentally cut, which will be quite painful for the dog as it contains nerve endings. Keep some type of clotting agent on hand, such as a styptic pencil or styptic powder (the type used for shaving). This will stop the bleeding quickly when applied

Your dog should be groomed on a grooming table that is adjusted to a comfortable working height for you. It should have a non-skid surface.

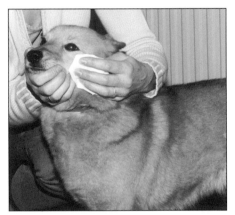

Keep the area around your Finnish Spitz's eyes clean by gently wiping with a soft cloth or cotton wipe. Pet shops also sell cleaning solutions for tear-stain removal that you may want to try.

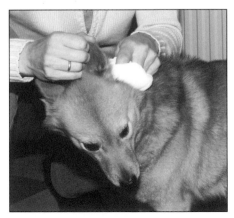

The ears are cleaned with a cotton ball or wipe and an ear powder or liquid made for dogs. *Never* enter the ear canal.

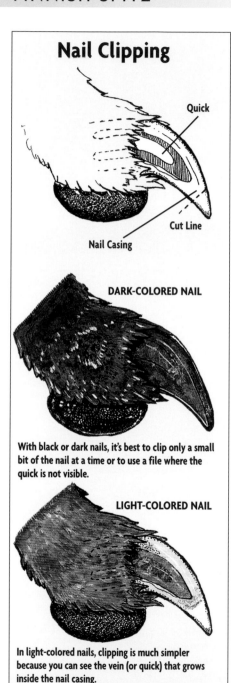

Nail Clipping

Quick

Cut Line

Nail Casing

DARK-COLORED NAIL

With black or dark nails, it's best to clip only a small bit of the nail at a time or to use a file where the quick is not visible.

LIGHT-COLORED NAIL

In light-colored nails, clipping is much simpler because you can see the vein (or quick) that grows inside the nail casing.

to the end of the cut nail. Do not panic if you cut the quick, just stop the bleeding and talk soothingly to your dog. Once he has calmed down, move on to the next nail. It is better to clip a little at a time, particularly with black-nailed dogs.

Hold your pup steady as you begin trimming his nails; you do not want him to make any sudden movements or run away. Talk to him soothingly and stroke him as you clip. Holding his foot in your hand, simply take off the end of each nail with one swift clip. You should purchase nail clippers that are made for use on dogs; there are several different types available and you can probably find them wherever you buy pet or grooming supplies.

TOOTH CARE
Teeth should always be kept clean and as free from tartar as possible. Your Finnish Spitz will have his teeth checked and possibly cleaned during his veterinary visits, but you should make home dental care part of your grooming routine. You can purchase special canine tooth-cleaning products, including small toothbrushes and toothpaste specially formulated for dogs.

TRAVELING WITH YOUR DOG

CAR TRAVEL
You should accustom your Finnish Spitz to riding in a car at an early age. You may or may not take him

in the car often, but at the very least he will need to go to the vet and you do not want these trips to be traumatic for the dog or troublesome for you. The safest way for a dog to ride in the car is in his crate. If he uses a crate in the house, you can use the same crate for travel.

Put the pup in the crate and see how he reacts. If he seems uneasy, you can have a passenger hold him on his lap while you drive. Another option for car travel is a specially made safety harness for dogs, which straps the dog in much like a seat belt. Do not let the dog roam loose in the vehicle—this is very dangerous! If you should stop short, your dog can be thrown and injured. If the dog starts climbing on you and pestering you while you are driving, you will not be able to concentrate on the road. It is an unsafe situation for everyone—human and canine.

Remember *never* to leave your dog alone in the car, even for a short amount of time. For long trips, bring along some water and be prepared to stop to let the dog relieve himself. Take with you whatever you need to clean up after him, including some paper towels and perhaps some old rags for use should he have a potty accident in the car or suffer from motion sickness.

AIR TRAVEL

Contact your chosen airline before proceeding with travel plans that

TRAVEL TIP
When traveling, never let your dog off-lead in a strange area. Your dog could run away out of fear, decide to chase a passing squirrel or cat or simply want to stretch his legs without restriction—if any of these happen, you might never see your canine friend again.

Never travel with your Finnish Spitz loose within the car. The safest place for your dog to be during car rides is secure in his crate.

Visit local boarding kennels before you need their services. Cost, cleanliness and convenience are just a few of the factors upon which you should base your decision. Also discuss boarding with your vet. Many vets offer boarding facilities or can recommend a good kennel.

include your Finnish Spitz. The dog will be required to travel in a fiberglass crate and you should always check in advance with the airline regarding specific requirements for the crate's size, type and labeling, as well as about any travel restrictions (such as during summer months) and health certifications needed for the dog.

To help put the dog at ease, give him one of his favorite toys in the crate. Do not feed the dog for several hours prior to checking in so that you minimize his need to relieve himself. Some airlines require you to provide documentation as to when the dog has last been fed. In any case, a light meal is best. For long trips, you will have to attach bowls for food and water, and a portion of food to the outside of the dog's crate so that

airline employees can tend to him between legs of the trip.

Make sure that your dog is properly identified and that your contact information appears on his ID tags and on his crate. Your Finnish Spitz will travel in a different area of the plane than the human passengers, so every rule must be strictly followed to prevent the risk of getting separated from your dog. Transporting animals is routine for large carriers, but you always want to play it safe.

VACATIONS AND BOARDING
So you want to take a family vacation—and you want to include *all* members of the family. You would probably make arrangements for accommodations ahead of time anyway, but this is

COLLAR REQUIRED

If your dog gets lost, he is not able to ask for directions home. Identification tags fastened to the collar give important information—the dog's name, the owner's name, the owner's address and a telephone number where the owner can be reached. This makes it easy for whoever finds the dog to contact the owner and arrange to have the dog returned. An added advantage is that a person will be more likely to approach a lost dog who has ID tags on his collar; it tells the person that this is somebody's pet rather than a stray. This is the easiest and fastest method of identification, provided that the tags stay on the collar and the collar stays on the dog.

especially important when traveling with a dog. You do not want to make an overnight stop at the only place around for miles, only to find out that they do not allow dogs. Also, you do not want to reserve a place for your family without confirming that you are traveling with a dog, because, if it is against the hotel's policy, you may end up without a place to stay.

Alternatively, if you are traveling and choose not to bring your Finnish Spitz, you will have to make arrangements for him while you are away. Some options are to take him to a friend's house to stay while you are gone, to have a trusted neighbor stay at your house or to bring your dog to a reputable boarding kennel. If you choose to board him at a kennel, you should visit in advance to see the facilities provided and where the dogs are kept. Are the dogs' areas spacious and kept clean? Talk to some of the employees and observe how they treat the dogs—do they spend time with the dogs, play with them, groom them, exercise them, etc.? Also find out the kennel's policy on vaccinations and what they require. This is for all of the dogs' safety, since there is a greater risk of diseases being passed from dog to dog when dogs are kept together.

IDENTIFICATION
Your Finnish Spitz is your valued companion and friend. That is why you always keep a close eye on him and you have made sure that he cannot escape from the yard or wriggle out of his collar and run away from you. However, accidents can happen and there may come a time when your dog unexpectedly becomes separated from you. If this unfortunate event should occur, the first thing on your mind will be finding him. Proper identification, including an ID tag, and possibly a tattoo and/or a microchip, will increase the chances of his being returned to you safely and quickly.

FINNISH SPITZ

Living with an untrained dog is a lot like owning a piano that you do not know how to play—it is a nice object to look at, but it does not do much more than that to bring you pleasure. Now try taking piano lessons, and suddenly the piano comes alive and brings forth magical sounds and rhythms that set your heart singing and your body swaying. The same is true with your Finnish Spitz. Any dog is a big responsibility and, if not trained sensibly, may develop unacceptable behavior that annoys you or could even cause family friction.

To train your Finnish Spitz, you may like to enroll in an obedience class. Teach your dog good manners as you learn how and why he behaves the way he does.

A puppy is a bundle of exuberance. It's fine to let a puppy be a puppy, but it's also your responsibility to channel that energy into mannerly behavior.

Find out how to communicate with your dog and how to recognize and understand his communications with you. Suddenly the dog takes on a new role in your life—he is clever, interesting, well behaved and fun to be with. He demonstrates his bond of devotion to you daily. In other words, your Finnish Spitz does wonders for your ego because he constantly reminds you that you are not only his leader, you are his hero!

Those involved with teaching dog obedience and counseling owners about their dogs' behavior have discovered some interesting facts about dog ownership. For example, training dogs when they are puppies results in the highest

EASY DOES IT
Gently laying your hand over the top of the dog's neck right behind the ears acts as a dominant signal. Adding a soothing, soft voice with the word "easy" can calm an overly excited dog and help him resume a normal attitude.

REAP THE REWARDS
If you start with a normal, healthy dog and give him time, patience and some carefully executed lessons, you will reap the rewards of that training for the life of the dog. And what a life it will be! The two of you will find immeasurable pleasure in the companionship you have built together with love, respect and understanding.

rate of success in developing well-mannered and well-adjusted adult dogs. Training an older dog, from six months to six years of age, can produce almost equal results, providing that the owner accepts the dog's slower rate of learning capability and is willing to work patiently to help the dog succeed at developing to his fullest potential. Unfortunately, many owners of untrained adult dogs lack the patience factor, so they do not persist until their dogs are successful at learning particular behaviors.

Training a puppy aged 10 to 16 weeks (20 weeks at the most) is like working with a dry sponge in a pool of water. The pup soaks up whatever you show him and constantly looks for more things to do and learn. At this early age, his body is not yet producing hormones, and therein lies the reason for such a high rate of success. Without hormones, he is focused on his owners and not particularly interested in investigating other places, dogs, people, etc. You are his leader, his provider of food, water, shelter and security. He latches onto you and wants to stay close. He will usually follow you from room to room, will not let you out of his sight when you are outdoors with him and will respond in like manner to the people and animals you encounter. If you greet a friend warmly, he will be happy

CALM DOWN

Dogs will do anything for your attention. If you reward the dog when he is calm and attentive, you will develop a well-mannered dog. If, on the other hand, you greet your dog excitedly and encourage him to wrestle with you, the dog will greet you the same way and you will have a hyperactive dog on your hands.

to greet the person as well. If, however, you are hesitant or anxious about the approach of a stranger, he will respond according to you.

Once the puppy begins to produce hormones, his natural curiosity emerges and he begins to investigate the world around him. It is at this time when you may notice that the untrained dog begins to wander away from you and even ignore your commands to stay close. When this behavior becomes a problem, you have two choices: get rid of the dog or train him. It is strongly urged that you choose the latter option.

You usually will be able to find obedience classes within a reasonable distance from your home, but you can also do a lot to train your dog yourself. Sometimes there are classes available, but the tuition is too costly. Whatever the circumstances, the solution to training your dog without formal obedience lessons lies within the pages of this book.

This chapter is devoted to helping you train your Finnish Spitz at home. If the recommended procedures are followed faithfully, you may expect positive results that will prove rewarding both to you and your dog. Whether your new charge is a puppy or a mature adult, the methods of teaching and the techniques we use in training basic behaviors are the same. After all, no dog, whether puppy or adult, likes harsh or inhumane methods. All creatures, however, respond favorably to gentle motivational methods and sincere praise and encouragement. Now let us get started.

HOUSEBREAKING

You can train a puppy to relieve himself wherever you choose, but this must be somewhere suitable. You should bear in mind from the

Multiple dogs mean multiple training. It would be impossible to control a group of dogs if each and every one had not been trained to behave politely and reliably.

commonly used by dog owners. Get in the habit of giving the puppy your chosen relief command before you take him out. That way, when he becomes an adult, you will be able to determine if he wants to go out when you ask him. A confirmation will be signs of interest, such as wagging his tail, watching you intently, going to the door, etc.

PUPPY'S NEEDS
Your puppy needs to relieve himself after play periods, after each meal, after he has been sleeping and at any time he indicates that he is looking for a place to urinate or defecate. The urinary and intestinal tract muscles of very young puppies are not fully developed. Therefore, like human babies, puppies need to relieve themselves frequently.

Take your puppy out often—every hour for an eight-week-old, for example—and always immediately after sleeping and eating. The older the puppy, the less often he will need to relieve

If you have intentions of showing, you will invest time in learning the ways of the ring and practicing with your dog. And what a wonderful reward for both of you when your hard work results in a prize!

outset that when your puppy is old enough to go out in public places, any canine deposits must be removed at once. You will always have to carry with you a small plastic bag or "poop-scoop."

Outdoor training includes such surfaces as grass, soil and cement. Indoor training usually means training your dog to newspaper. When deciding on the surface and location that you will want your Finnish Spitz to use, be sure it is going to be permanent. Training your dog to grass and then changing your mind a few months later is extremely difficult for both dog and owner.

Next, choose the command you will use each and every time you want your puppy to relieve himself. "Hurry up" and "Let's go" are examples of commands

PARENTAL GUIDANCE
Training a dog is a life experience. Many parents admit that much of what they know about raising children they learned from caring for their dogs. Dogs respond to love, fairness and guidance, just as children do. Become a good dog owner and you may become an even better parent.

SAFETY FIRST

While it may seem that the most important things to your dog are eating, sleeping and chewing the upholstery on your furniture, his first concern is actually safety. The domesticated dogs we keep as companions have the same pack instinct as their ancestors who ran free thousands of years ago. Because of this pack instinct, your dog wants to know that he and his pack are not in danger of being harmed, and that his pack has a strong, capable leader. You must establish yourself as the leader early on in your relationship. That way your dog will trust that you will take care of him and the pack, and he will accept your commands without question.

himself. Finally, as a mature healthy adult, he will require only three to five relief trips per day.

HOUSING

Since the types of housing and control you provide for your puppy have a direct relationship on the success of house-training, we consider the various aspects of both before we begin training. Taking a new puppy home and turning him loose in your house can be compared to turning a child loose in a sports arena and telling the child that the place is all his! The sheer enormity of the place would be too much for him to handle.

Instead, offer the puppy clearly defined areas where he can play, sleep, eat and live. A room of the house where the family gathers is the most obvious choice. Puppies are social animals and need to feel a part of the pack right from the start. Hearing your voice, watching you while you are doing things and smelling you nearby are all positive reinforcers that he is now a member of your pack. Usually a family room, the kitchen or a nearby adjoining breakfast area is ideal for providing safety and security for both puppy and owner.

Within the designated room, there should be a smaller area that the puppy can call his own. An alcove, a wire or fiberglass dog crate or a gated (not boarded!) corner from which he can view the activities of his new family

If you have a fenced-in yard, lead your puppy to an out-of-the way area in the yard for his relief area. It's normal for him to sniff around a bit until he picks a pleasing spot.

CANINE DEVELOPMENT SCHEDULE

It is important to understand how and at what age a puppy develops into adulthood.
If you are a puppy owner, consult the following Canine Development Schedule to
determine the stage of development your puppy is currently experiencing.
This knowledge will help you as you work with the puppy in the weeks and months ahead.

Period	Age	Characteristics
FIRST TO THIRD	BIRTH TO SEVEN WEEKS	Puppy needs food, sleep and warmth, and responds to simple and gentle touching. Needs mother for security and disciplining. Needs littermates for learning and interacting with other dogs. Pup learns to function within a pack and learns pack order of dominance. Begin socializing pup with adults and children for short periods. Pup begins to become aware of his environment.
FOURTH	EIGHT TO TWELVE WEEKS	Brain is fully developed. Needs socializing with outside world. Remove from mother and littermates. Needs to change from canine pack to human pack. Human dominance necessary. Fear period occurs between 8 and 12 weeks. Avoid fright and pain.
FIFTH	THIRTEEN TO SIXTEEN WEEKS	Training and formal obedience should begin. Less association with other dogs, more with people, places, situations. Period will pass easily if you remember this is pup's change-to-adolescence time. Be firm and fair. Flight instinct prominent. Permissiveness and over-disciplining can do permanent damage. Praise for good behavior.
JUVENILE	FOUR TO EIGHT MONTHS	Another fear period about 7 to 8 months of age. It passes quickly, but be cautious of fright and pain. Sexual maturity reached. Dominant traits established. Dog should understand sit, down, come and stay by now.

NOTE: THESE ARE APPROXIMATE TIME FRAMES. ALLOW FOR INDIVIDUAL DIFFERENCES IN PUPPIES.

will be fine. The size of the area or crate is the key factor here. The area must be large enough so that the puppy can lie down and stretch out, as well as stand up, without rubbing his head on the top. At the same time, it must be small enough so that he cannot relieve himself at one end and sleep at the other without coming into contact with his droppings. Dogs are, by nature, clean animals and will not remain close to their relief areas unless forced to do so. In those cases, they then become dirty dogs and usually remain that way for life.

The dog's designated area should contain clean bedding and a toy. Once your Finnish Spitz is housebroken reliably, water must always be available in his area, in a non-spill container. During the housebreaking process, putting food or water in the dog's crate will defeat your purposes as well as make the puppy very uncomfortable as he tries to "hold it."

CONTROL

By *control*, we mean helping the puppy to create a lifestyle pattern that will be compatible to that of his human pack (you!). Just as we guide little children to learn our way of life, we must show the puppy when it is time to play, eat, sleep, exercise and even entertain himself.

Your puppy should always sleep in his crate. He should also learn that, during times of household confusion and excessive human activity, such as at breakfast when family members are preparing for the day, he can play by himself in relative safety and comfort in his designated area. Each time you leave the puppy alone, he should understand exactly where he is to stay.

Puppies are chewers and cannot tell the difference between

Potty time or play time? Don't let your pup become distracted from the task at hand. Encourage him to do his duty right away, and then allow time for play.

things like lamp and television cords, shoes, table legs, etc. Chewing into a television wire, for example, can be fatal to the puppy, while a shorted wire can start a fire in the house. In a different scenario, if the puppy chews on the arm of the chair when he is alone, you will probably discipline him angrily when you get home. Thus, he makes the association that your coming home means he is going to be punished. (He will not remember chewing the chair and is incapable of making the association of the discipline with his naughty deed.) Accustoming the pup to his

If you have a tree in your yard, your Finnish Spitz may just decide that it makes a good bathroom!

HOW MANY TIMES A DAY?

AGE	RELIEF TRIPS
To 14 weeks	10
14–22 weeks	8
22–32 weeks	6
Adulthood (dog stops growing)	4

These are estimates, of course, but they are a guide to the *minimum* number of opportunities a dog should have each day to relieve himself.

crate not only keeps him safe but also avoids his engaging in dangerous or destructive behaviors when you are not around to supervise.

Times of excitement, such as special occasions, family parties, etc., can be fun for the puppy, providing that he can view the activities from the security of his designated area. He is not underfoot and he is not being fed all sorts of tidbits that will probably cause him stomach distress, yet he still feels a part of the fun. The aforementioned situations illustrate just some of the ways in which crate training can be useful for keeping your dog safe and encouraging good behavior by keeping him out of trouble.

ESTABLISHING A SCHEDULE

Your puppy should be taken to his relief area each time he is released from his designated area, after meals, after play sessions and when he first awakens in the morning (at age eight weeks, this can mean 5 a.m.!). The puppy will indicate that he's ready "to go" by circling or sniffing busily—do not misinterpret these signs. For a puppy of less than ten weeks of age, a routine of taking him out every hour is necessary. As the puppy grows, he will be able to wait for longer periods of time.

Keep trips to his relief area short. Stay no more than five or six minutes and then return to the house. If he goes during that time, praise him lavishly and take him indoors immediately. If he does not, but he has an accident when you go back indoors, pick him up immediately, say "No! No!" and return to his relief area. Wait a few minutes, then return to the house again. Never hit a puppy or put his face in urine or excrement when he has had an accident!

Once indoors, put the puppy in his crate until you have had time to clean up his accident. Then, release him to the family area and watch him more closely than before. Chances are, his accident was a result of your not picking up his signal or waiting too long before offering him the opportunity to relieve himself. Never hold a grudge against the puppy for accidents.

Let the puppy learn that going outdoors means it is time to relieve himself, not to play. Once

HOUSE-TRAINING TIP
Most of all, be consistent. Always take your dog to the same location, always use the same command and always have the dog on lead when he is in his relief area, unless a fenced-in yard is available.

By following the method described in this chapter, your puppy will be completely housebroken by the time his muscle and brain development reach maturity. Keep in mind that small breeds usually mature faster than large breeds, but all puppies should be trained by six months of age.

trained, he will be able to play indoors and out and still differentiate between the times for play versus the times for relief. Help him develop regular hours for naps, being alone, playing by himself and just resting, all in his crate. Encourage him to entertain himself while you are busy with your activities. Let him learn that having you near is comforting, but it is not your main purpose in life to provide him with undivided attention.

Each time you put your puppy in his own area, use the same command, whatever suits best. Soon he will run to his crate or special area when he hears you say those words. Crate training provides safety for you, the puppy and the home. It also provides the puppy with a feeling of security, and that helps the puppy achieve self-confidence and clean habits. Remember that one of the primary ingredients in house-training your

THE SUCCESS METHOD

Success that comes by luck is usually short-lived. Success that comes by well-thought-out proven methods is often more easily achieved and permanent. This is the Success Method. It is designed to give you, the puppy owner, a simple yet proven way to help your puppy develop clean living habits and a feeling of security in his new environment.

6 Steps to Successful Crate Training

1 Tell the puppy "Crate time!" and place him in the crate with a small treat (a piece of cheese or half of a biscuit). Let him stay in the crate for five minutes while you are in the same room. Then release him and praise lavishly. Never release him when he is fussing. Wait until he is quiet before you let him out.

2 Repeat Step 1 several times a day.

3 The next day, place the puppy in the crate as before. Let him stay there for ten minutes. Do this several times.

4 Continue building time in five-minute increments until the puppy stays in his crate for 30 minutes with you in the room. Always take him to his relief area after prolonged periods in his crate.

5 Now go back to Step 1 and let the puppy stay in his crate for five minutes, this time while you are out of the room.

6 Once again, build crate time in five-minute increments with you out of the room. When the puppy will stay willingly in his crate (he may even fall asleep!) for 30 minutes with you out of the room, he will be ready to stay in it for several hours at a time.

puppy is control. Regardless of your lifestyle, there will always be occasions when you will need to have a place where your dog can stay and be happy and safe. Crate training is the answer for now and in the future.

In conclusion, a few key elements are really all you need for a successful housebreaking method—consistency, frequency, praise, control and supervision. By following these procedures with a normal, healthy puppy, you and the puppy will soon be past the stage of "accidents" and ready to move on to a clean and rewarding life together.

ROLES OF DISCIPLINE, REWARD AND PUNISHMENT

Discipline, training one to act in accordance with rules, brings order to life. It is as simple as that. Without discipline, particularly in a group society, chaos will reign supreme and the group will eventually perish. Humans and canines are social animals and need some form of discipline in order to function effectively. They must procure food, protect their home base and their young and reproduce to keep their species going. If there were no discipline in the lives of social animals, they would eventually die from starvation and/or predation by stronger animals.

In the case of domestic canines, discipline in their lives is

CONSISTENCY PAYS OFF
Dogs need consistency in their feeding schedule, exercise and relief visits, and in the verbal commands you use. If you use "Stay" on Monday and "Stay here, please" on Tuesday, you will confuse your dog. Don't demand perfect behavior during training sessions and then let him have the run of the house the rest of the day. Above all, lavish praise on your pet consistently every time he does something right. The more he feels he is pleasing you, the more willing he will be to learn.

needed in order for them to understand how their pack (you and other family members) functions and how they must act in order to survive. A large humane society in a highly populated area recently surveyed dog owners regarding their satisfaction with

TRAINING RULES

If you want to be successful in training your dog, you have four rules to obey yourself:
1. Develop an understanding of how a dog thinks.
2. Do not blame the dog for lack of communication.
3. Define your dog's personality and act accordingly.
4. Have patience and be consistent.

their relationships with their dogs. People who had trained their dogs were 75% more satisfied with their pets than those who had never trained their dogs.

Dr. Edward Thorndike, a noted psychologist, established *Thorndike's Theory of Learning,* which states that a behavior that results in a pleasant event tends to be repeated. Furthermore, it concludes that a behavior that results in an unpleasant event

The first step in any type of training is getting and keeping the dog's attention.

tends not to be repeated. It is this theory upon which training methods are based today. For example, if you manipulate a dog to perform a specific behavior and reward him for doing it, he is likely to do it again because he enjoyed the end result.

Occasionally, punishment, a penalty inflicted for an offense, is necessary. The best type of punishment often comes from an outside source. For example, a child is told not to touch the stove because he may get burned. He disobeys and touches the stove. In doing so, he receives a burn. From that time on, he respects the heat of the stove and avoids contact with it. Therefore, a behavior that results in an unpleasant event tends not to be repeated.

A good example of a dog's learning the hard way is the dog who chases the house cat. He is told many times to leave the cat alone, yet he persists in teasing the cat. Then, one day, the dog begins chasing the cat but the cat turns and swipes a claw across the dog's face, leaving the dog with a painful gash on his nose. The final result is that the dog stops chasing the cat.

TRAINING EQUIPMENT

Collar and Leash

For a Finnish Spitz, the collar and leash that you use for training must be one with which you are

easily able to work, not too heavy for the dog and perfectly safe.

TREATS

Have a bag of treats on hand; something nutritious and easy to swallow works best. Use a soft treat, a chunk of cheese or a piece of cooked chicken rather than a dry biscuit. By the time the dog has finished chewing a dry treat, he will forget why he is being rewarded in the first place!

As a sidebar, using food rewards will not teach a dog to beg at the table—the only way to teach a dog to beg at the table is to give him food from the table. In training, rewarding the dog with a food treat will help him associate praise and the treats with learning new behaviors that obviously please his owner.

TRAINING BEGINS: ASK THE DOG A QUESTION

In order to teach your dog anything, you must first get his attention. After all, he cannot learn anything if he is looking away from you with his mind on something else. To get your dog's attention, ask him "School?" and immediately walk over to him and give him a treat as you tell him "Good dog." Wait a minute or two and repeat the routine, this time with a treat in your hand as you approach within a foot of the dog. Do not go directly to him, but stop about a foot short of him and hold

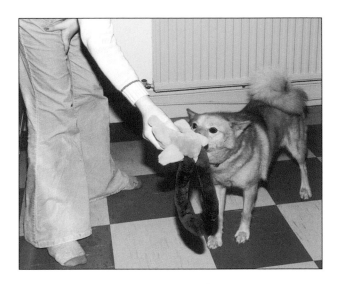

out the treat as you ask "School?" He will see you approaching with a treat in your hand and most likely begin walking toward you. As you meet, give him the treat and praise again.

The third time, ask the question, have a treat in your hand and walk only a short distance toward the dog so that he must walk almost all the way to you. As he reaches you, give him the

Don't be all work and no play! Take a break from your training to have fun with your dog.

LANGUAGE BARRIER

Dogs do not understand our language and have to rely on tone of voice more than just words or sound. They can be trained to react to a certain sound, at a certain volume. If you say "No, Oliver" in a very soft, pleasant voice, it will not have the same meaning as "No, Oliver!!" when you raise your voice.

treat and praise again. By this time, the dog will probably be getting the idea that if he pays attention to you, especially when you ask that question, it will pay off in treats and enjoyable activities for him. In other words, he learns that "school" means doing great things with you that are fun and that result in positive attention for him.

Remember that the dog does not understand your verbal language; he only recognizes sounds. Your question translates to a series of sounds for him, and those sounds become the signal to go to you and pay attention. The dog learns that if he does this, he will get to interact with you plus receive treats and praise.

THE BASIC COMMANDS

TEACHING SIT

Now that you have the dog's attention, attach his leash and hold it in your left hand, and hold a food treat in your right hand. Place your food hand at the dog's nose and let him lick the treat but not take it from you. Say "Sit" and slowly raise your food hand from in front of the dog's nose up over his head so that he is looking at the ceiling. As he bends his head upward, he will have to bend his knees to maintain his balance. As he bends his knees, he will assume a sit position. At that point, release the food treat

and praise lavishly with comments such as "Good dog! Good sit!," etc. Remember to always praise enthusiastically, because dogs relish verbal praise from their owners and feel so proud of themselves whenever they accomplish a behavior.

Incidentally, you will not use food forever in getting the dog to obey your commands. Food is only used to teach new behaviors and, once the dog knows what you want when you give a specific command, you will wean him off food treats but still maintain verbal praise. After all, you will always have your voice with you, and there will be many times when you have no food rewards but expect the dog to obey.

TEACHING DOWN

Teaching the down exercise is easy when you understand how the dog perceives the down position, and it is very difficult when you do not. Dogs perceive the down position as a submissive one; therefore, teaching the down exercise by using a forceful method can sometimes make the dog develop such a fear of the down that he either runs away when you say "Down" or attempts to snap at the person who tries to force him down.

Have the dog sit close alongside your left leg, facing in the same direction as you are. Hold the leash in your left hand and a

Sit is a very basic command, and likely the first one you will teach. It serves as a foundation for further exercises.

DOUBLE JEOPARDY

A dog in jeopardy never lies down. He stays alert on his feet because instinct tells him that he may have to run away or fight for his survival. Therefore, if a dog feels threatened or anxious, he will not lie down. Consequently, it is important to keep the dog calm and relaxed as he learns the down exercise.

food treat in your right. Now place your left hand lightly on the top of the dog's shoulders where they meet above the spinal cord. Do not push down on the dog's shoulders; simply rest your left hand there so you can guide the dog to lie down close to your left leg rather than to swing away from your side when he drops.

Now place the food hand at the dog's nose, say "Down" very softly (almost a whisper) and

slowly lower the food hand to the dog's front feet. When the food hand reaches the floor, begin moving it forward along the floor in front of the dog. Keep talking softly to the dog, saying things like, "Do you want this treat? You can do this, good dog." Your reassuring tone of voice will help calm the dog as he tries to follow the food hand in order to get the treat.

When the dog's elbows touch the floor, release the food and praise softly. Try to get the dog to maintain that down position for several seconds before you let him sit up again. The goal here is to get the dog to settle down and not feel threatened in the down position.

TEACHING STAY

It is easy to teach the dog to stay in either a sit or a down position. Again, we use food and praise during the teaching process as we help the dog to understand exactly what it is that we are expecting him to do.

To teach the sit/stay, start with the dog sitting on your left side as before and hold the leash in your left hand. Have a food treat in your right hand and place your food hand at the dog's nose. Say "Stay" and step out on your right foot to stand directly in front of the dog, toe to toe, as he licks and nibbles the treat. Be sure to keep his head facing upward to maintain the sit position. Count to five and then swing around to stand next to the dog again with him on your left. As soon as you get back to the original position, release the food and praise lavishly.

To teach the down/stay, do the down as previously described. As soon as the dog lies down, say "Stay" and step out on your right foot just as you did in the sit/stay. Count to five and then return to stand beside the dog with him on your left side. Release the treat and praise as always.

Within a week or ten days, you can begin to add a bit of distance between you and your dog when you leave him. When you do, use your left hand open

PRACTICE MAKES PERFECT!

• Have training lessons with your dog every day in several short segments—three to five times a day for a few minutes at a time is ideal.

• Do not have long practice sessions. The dog will become easily bored.

• Never practice when you are tired, ill, worried or in an otherwise negative mood. This will transmit to the dog and may have an adverse effect on his performance.

Think fun, short and above all *positive!* End each session on a high note, rather than a failed exercise, and make sure to give a lot of praise. Enjoy the training and help your dog enjoy it, too.

with the palm facing the dog as a stay signal, much the same as the hand signal a police officer uses to stop traffic at an intersection. Hold the food treat in your right hand as before, but this time the food will not be touching the dog's nose. He will watch the food hand and quickly learn that he is going to get that treat as soon as you return to his side.

When you can stand 3 feet away from your dog for 30 seconds, you can then begin building time and distance in both stays. Eventually, the dog can be expected to remain in the stay position for prolonged periods of time until you return to him or call him to you. Always praise lavishly when he stays.

TEACHING COME

If you make teaching "come" an exciting experience, you should never have a student that does not love the game or that fails to come when called. The secret, it seems, is never to teach the word "come."

At times when an owner most wants his dog to come when called, the owner is likely to be upset or anxious, and he allows these feelings to come through in the tone of his voice when he calls his dog. Hearing that desperation in his owner's voice, the dog fears the results of going to him and therefore either disobeys outright or runs in the opposite

"COME" . . . BACK

Never call your dog to come to you for a correction or scold him when he reaches you. That is the quickest way to turn a come command into "Go away fast!" Dogs think only in the present tense, and your dog will connect the scolding with coming to you, not with the misbehavior of a few moments earlier.

direction. The secret, therefore, is to teach the dog a game and, when you want him to come to you, simply play the game. It is practically a no-fail solution!

To begin, have several members of your family take a few food treats and each go into a different room in the house. Everyone takes turns calling the dog, and each person should celebrate the dog's finding him with a treat and lots of happy praise. When a person calls the dog, he is actually inviting the dog to find him and to get a treat as a reward for "winning."

A few turns of the "Where are you?" game and the dog will understand that everyone is playing the game and that each person has a big celebration awaiting the dog's success at locating him or her. Once the dog learns to love the game, simply calling out "Where are you?" will bring him running from wherever he is when he hears that all-important question.

The come command is recognized as one of the most important things to teach a dog, but there are trainers who work with thousands of dogs and never use the actual word "come." Yet these dogs will race to respond to a person who uses the dog's name followed by "Where are you?" For example, a woman has a 12-year-old companion dog who went blind, but who never fails to locate her owner when asked "Where are you?"

Children, in particular, love to play this game with their dogs. Children can hide in smaller places like a shower or bathtub, behind a bed or under a table. The dog needs to work a little bit harder to find these hiding places, but, when he does, he loves to celebrate with a treat and a tussle with a favorite youngster.

TEACHING HEEL

Heeling means that the dog walks beside the owner without pulling. It takes time and patience on the owner's part to succeed at teaching the dog that he (the owner) will not proceed unless the dog is walking calmly beside him. Neither pulling out ahead on the leash nor lagging behind is acceptable.

Begin by holding the leash in your left hand as the dog sits beside your left leg. Move the loop end of the leash to your right hand, but keep your left hand short on the leash so that it keeps the dog in close next to you. Say "Heel" and step forward on your left foot. Keep the dog close to you and take three steps. Stop and have the dog sit next to you in what we now call the heel position. Praise verbally, but do not touch the dog. Hesitate a moment and begin again with "Heel," taking three steps and stopping, at which point the dog is told to sit again.

"WHERE ARE YOU?"
When calling the dog, do not say "Come." Say things like, "Rover, where are you? See if you can find me! I have a biscuit for you!" Keep up a constant line of chatter with coaxing sounds and frequent questions such as, "Where are you?" The dog will learn to follow the sound of your voice to locate you and receive his reward.

Your goal here is to have the dog walk those three steps without pulling on the leash. Once he will walk calmly beside you for three steps without pulling, increase the number of steps you take to five. When he will walk politely beside you while you take five steps, you can increase the length of your walk to ten steps. Keep increasing

COMMAND STANCE

Stand up straight and authoritatively when giving your dog commands. Do not issue commands when lying on the floor or lying on your back on the sofa. If you are on your hands and knees when you give a command, your dog will think you are positioning yourself to play.

the length of your stroll until the dog will walk quietly beside you without pulling as long as you want him to heel. When you stop heeling, indicate to the dog that the exercise is over by verbally praising as you pet him and say "OK, good dog." The "OK" is used as a release word, meaning that the exercise is finished and the dog is free to relax.

If you are dealing with a dog who insists on pulling you around, simply "put on your brakes" and stand your ground until the dog realizes that the two of you are not going anywhere until he is beside you and moving at your pace, not his. It may take some time just standing there to convince the dog that you are the leader and that you will be the one to decide on the direction and speed of your travel.

Each time the dog looks up at you or slows down to give a slack leash between the two of you, quietly praise him and say, "Good heel. Good dog." Eventually, the dog will begin to respond and within a few days he will be walking politely beside you without pulling on the leash. At first, the training sessions should be kept short and very positive; soon the dog will be able to walk nicely with you for increasingly longer distances. Remember also to give the dog free time and the opportunity to run and play when you have finished heel practice.

WEANING OFF FOOD IN TRAINING

Food is used in training new behaviors. Once the dog understands what behavior goes with a specific command, it is time to start weaning him off the food treats. At first, give a treat after each exercise. Then, start to give a treat only after every other exercise. Mix up the times when you offer a food reward and the times when you offer only praise so that the dog will never know when he is going to receive both food and praise and when he is going to receive only praise. This is called a variable-ratio reward system. It proves successful because there is always the chance that the owner will produce a treat, so the dog never stops trying for that reward. No matter what, *always* give verbal praise.

OBEDIENCE CLASSES

It is a good idea to enroll in an obedience class if one is available

The premise of heeling is that the dog must learn to adjust the speed of his gait to that of his owner. The dog goes where his owner goes, not the other way around!

in your area. If yours is a show dog, handling classes would be more appropriate. Many areas have dog clubs that offer basic obedience training as well as preparatory classes for obedience competition. There are also local dog trainers who offer similar classes. The Finnish Spitz, as a rule, does not usually make a very successful obedience competitor, although there are doubtless a few exceptions! Finnish Spitzen get bored with repetition and frequently like to add their own variations to the training program!

At obedience trials, dogs can earn titles at various levels of competition. The beginning levels of obedience competition include basic behaviors such as sit, down, heel, etc. The more advanced levels of competition include

---

TUG OF WALK?

If you begin teaching the heel by taking long walks and letting the dog pull you along, he misinterprets this action as an acceptable form of taking a walk. When you pull back on the leash to counteract his pulling, he reads that tug as a signal to pull even harder! Be consistent in encouraging your dog's polite behavior on lead.

HOW TO WEAN THE "TREAT HOG"

If you have trained your dog by rewarding him with a treat each time he performs a command, he may soon decide that without the treat, he won't sit, stay or come. The best way to fix this problem is to start asking your dog to do certain commands twice before being rewarded. Slowly increase the number of commands given and then vary the number: three sits and a treat one day, five sits for a biscuit the next day, etc. Your dog will soon realize that there is no set number of sits before he gets his reward and he'll likely do it the first time you ask in the hope of being rewarded sooner rather than later.

jumping, retrieving, scent discrimination and signal work. The advanced levels require a dog and owner to put a lot of time and effort into their training. The titles that can be earned at these levels of competition are very prestigious.

OTHER ACTIVITIES FOR LIFE
Whether a dog is trained in the structured environment of a class or alone with his owner at home, there are many activities that can bring fun and rewards to both owner and dog once they have mastered basic control. Of course, with the Finnish Spitz, hunting is always an option. With proper training, your dog will enjoy the chance to participate in the activity for which he was intended and to hone his natural instincts.

Teaching the dog to help out around the home, in the yard or on the farm provides great satisfaction to both dog and owner. In addition, the dog's help makes life a little easier for his owner and raises his stature as a valued companion to his family. It helps give the dog a purpose by occupying his mind and providing an outlet for his energy.

Backpacking is an exciting and healthy activity that the dog can be taught without assistance from more than his owner. The exercise of walking and climbing is good for man and dog alike, and

the bond that they develop together is priceless. The rule for backpacking with any dog is never to expect the dog to carry more than one-sixth of his body weight.

If you are interested in participating in organized competition with your Finnish Spitz, there are activities other than obedience in which you and your dog can become involved. Agility is a popular sport in which dogs run through obstacle courses that include various jumps, tunnels and other exercises to test the dog's speed and coordination. The owners run beside their dogs to give commands and to guide them through the course. Although competitive, the focus is on fun— it's fun to do, fun to watch and great exercise.

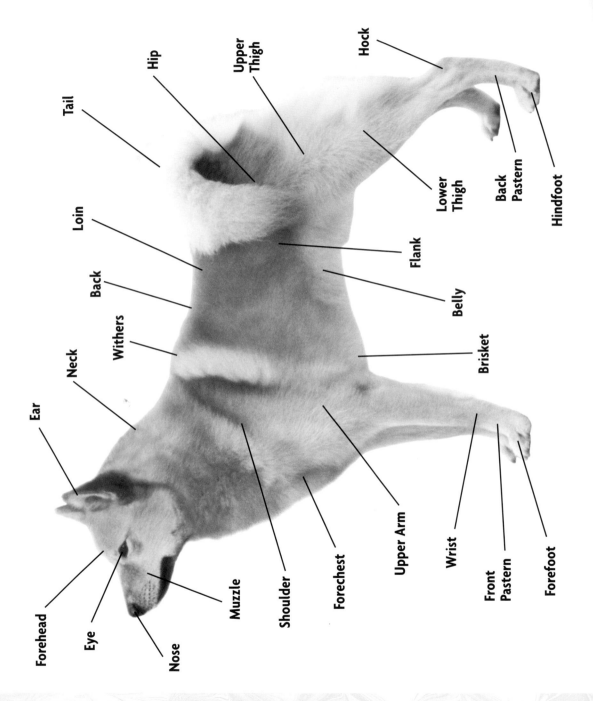

PHYSICAL STRUCTURE OF THE FINNISH SPITZ

FINNISH SPITZ

Dogs suffer from many of the same physical illnesses as people and might even share many of the same psychological problems. Since people usually know more about human diseases than canine maladies, many of the terms used in this chapter will be familiar but not necessarily those used by vets. For example, we will use the familiar term "x-ray" instead of "radiograph." We will also use the familiar term "symptoms," even though dogs don't have symptoms, which are verbal descriptions of something the patient feels or observes himself that he regards as abnormal. Dogs have "clinical signs" since they cannot speak, so we have to look for these clinical signs…but we still use the term "symptoms" in the book.

Medicine is a constantly changing art, of course with scientific input as well. Things alter as we learn more and more about basic sciences such as genetics and biochemistry, and have use of more sophisticated imaging techniques like Computer Aided Tomography (CAT scans) and Magnetic Resonance Imaging (MRI scans). There is academic dispute about many canine maladies, so different vets treat them in different ways; for example, some vets place a greater emphasis on surgical techniques than others.

SELECTING A QUALIFIED VET
Your selection of a veterinarian should be based on his reputation and skills with small animals, especially dogs, and, if possible, especially spitz breeds. If the vet is based nearby, it will be helpful because you might have an emergency or need to make multiple visits for treatments.

All vets should be licensed and capable of dealing with routine medical issues such as infections, injuries, routine surgeries (such as neutering) and the promotion of health (for example, by vaccination). If the problem affecting your dog is more complex, your vet will refer your pet to someone with a more detailed knowledge of what is wrong. This will usually be a specialist at the nearest university veterinary school who concentrates in the field relevant to your dog's ailment (veterinary derma-

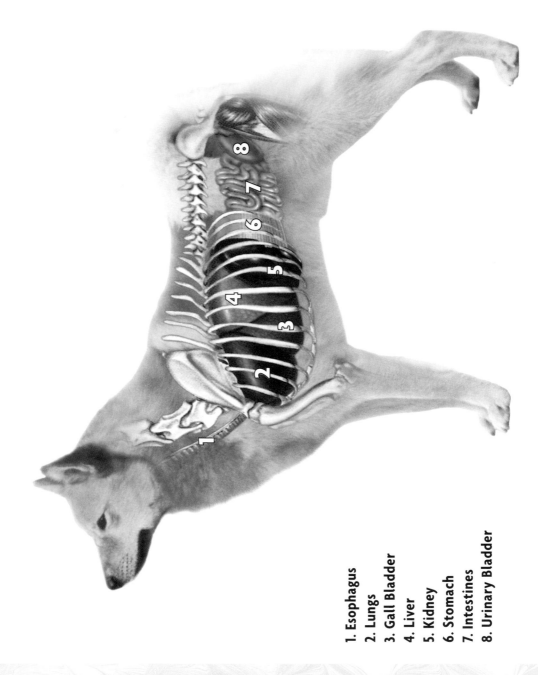

1. Esophagus
2. Lungs
3. Gall Bladder
4. Liver
5. Kidney
6. Stomach
7. Intestines
8. Urinary Bladder

INTERNAL ORGANS OF THE FINNISH SPITZ

tology, veterinary ophthalmology, veterinary cardiology, etc.).

Veterinary procedures are very costly and, as the treatments available improve, they are going to become more expensive. It is quite acceptable to discuss matters of cost with your vet; if there is more than one treatment option, cost may be a factor in deciding which route to take. It also is acceptable to get a second opinion, although it is courteous to advise the vets concerned.

Insurance against veterinary cost is also becoming very popular. The range of options available for your dog's health-care coverage is almost comparable to that for your own! Basic policies will cover the costs for unexpected emergencies such as emergency surgery after an accident, while more extensive (and expensive) coverage includes routine care, vaccinations, etc.

PREVENTATIVE MEDICINE

It is much easier, less costly and more effective to practice preventative medicine than to fight bouts of illness and disease. Properly bred puppies of all breeds come from parents that were selected based upon their genetic-disease profiles. The puppies' mother should have been vaccinated, free of all internal and external parasites and properly nourished. For these reasons, a visit to the vet who cared for the dam is recom-

Breakdown of Veterinary Income by Category

2%	Dentistry
4%	Radiology
12%	Surgery
15%	Vaccinations
19%	Laboratory
23%	Examinations
25%	Medicines

A typical vet's income, categorized according to services performed. This survey dealt with small-animal (pets) practices.

mended if at all possible. The dam passes disease resistance to her puppies, which should last from eight to ten weeks. Unfortunately, she can also pass on parasites and infection. This is why knowledge about her health is useful in learning more about the health of the puppies.

WEANING TO BRINGING PUP HOME
Puppies should be weaned by the time they are two months old. A puppy that remains for at least eight weeks with his mother and littermates usually adapts better to other dogs and people later in life.

Sometimes new owners have their puppy examined by a vet immediately, which is a good idea unless the puppy is overtired by a long journey home from the breeder's. In that case, an appointment for the pup should be arranged for the next day.

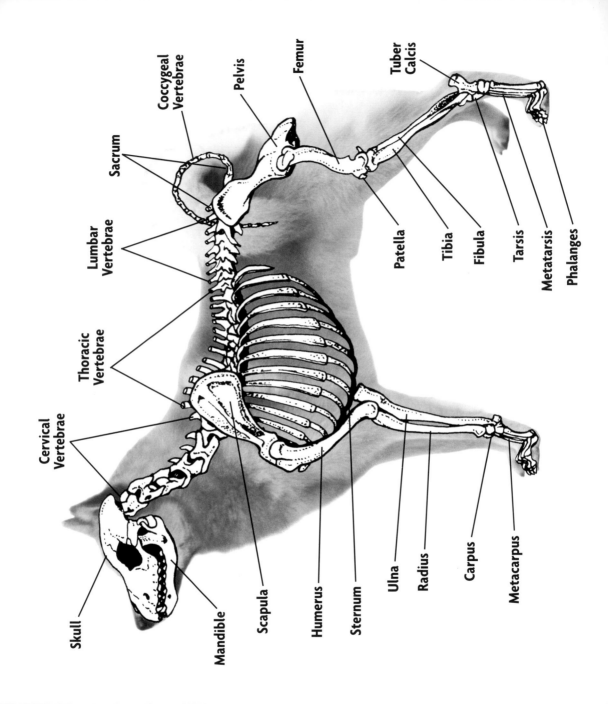

Coccygeal Vertebrae

Pelvis

Femur

Tuber Calcis

Sacrum

Lumbar Vertebrae

Thoracic Vertebrae

Cervical Vertebrae

Patella

Tibia

Fibula

Tarsis

Metatarsis

Phalanges

Skull

Mandible

Scapula

Humerus

Sternum

Ulna

Radius

Carpus

Metacarpus

SKELETAL STRUCTURE OF THE FINNISH SPITZ

The puppy will have his teeth examined and have his skeletal conformation and general health checked prior to certification by the vet. Puppies in certain breeds have problems with their kneecaps, cataracts and other eye problems, heart murmurs and undescended testicles. Your vet might also have training in temperament testing and evaluation. In addition, at the first visit, the vet will set up a schedule for the puppy's vaccinations.

VACCINATIONS
Most vaccinations are given by injection and should only be given by a vet. Both he and you should keep a record of the date of the injection, the identification of the vaccine and the amount given. Some vets give a first vaccination at six weeks, but most dog breeders prefer the course not to commence until about eight weeks because of the risk of interaction with the antibodies produced by the mother. The vaccination schedule is usually based on a two- to four-week cycle. You must take your vet's advice as to when to vaccinate, as this may differ according to the vaccine used.

The usual vaccines contain

HEALTH AND VACCINATION SCHEDULE

AGE IN WEEKS:	6TH	8TH	10TH	12TH	14TH	16TH	20-24TH	52ND
Worm Control	✔	✔	✔	✔	✔	✔	✔	
Neutering							✔	
Heartworm		✔		✔		✔	✔	
Parvovirus	✔		✔		✔		✔	✔
Distemper		✔		✔		✔		✔
Hepatitis		✔		✔		✔		✔
Leptospirosis								✔
Parainfluenza	✔		✔		✔			✔
Dental Examination		✔					✔	✔
Complete Physical		✔					✔	✔
Coronavirus				✔			✔	✔
Canine Cough	✔							
Hip Dysplasia							✔	
Rabies							✔	

Vaccinations are not instantly effective. It takes about two weeks for the dog's immune system to develop antibodies. Most vaccinations require annual booster shots. Your vet should guide you in this regard.

immunizing doses of several different viruses such as distemper, parvovirus, parainfluenza and hepatitis. There are other vaccines available when the puppy is at risk. You should rely upon professional advice. This is especially true for the booster immunizations. Most vaccination programs require a booster when the puppy is a year old and once a year thereafter. In some cases, circumstances may require more or less frequent immunizations.

Kennel or canine cough, more formally known as tracheobronchitis, is immunized against with a vaccine that is sprayed into the dog's nostrils. Canine cough is usually included in routine vaccination, but it is often not as effective as the vaccines for other major diseases.

FIVE MONTHS TO ONE YEAR OF AGE

Unless you intend to breed or show your dog, neutering the puppy around six months of age is recommended. Discuss this with your vet. Neutering and spaying have proven to be extremely beneficial to male and female dogs, respectively. Besides eliminating the possibility of pregnancy and

Normal hairs of a dog enlarged 200 times original size. The cuticle (outer covering) is clean and healthy. Unlike human hair that grows from the base, a dog's hair also grows from the end. Damaged hairs and split ends, illustrated above.

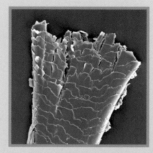
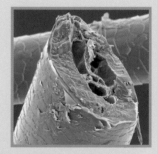
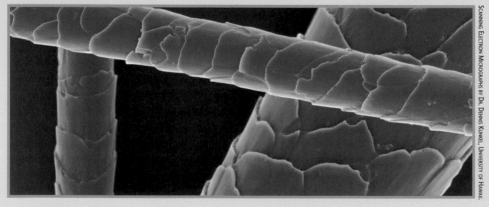

SCANNING ELECTRON MICROGRAPHS BY DR. DENNIS KUNKEL, UNIVERSITY OF HAWAII.

DISEASE REFERENCE CHART

	What is it?	What causes it?	Symptoms
Leptospirosis	Severe disease that affects the internal organs; can be spread to people.	A bacterium, which is often carried by rodents, that enters through mucous membranes and spreads quickly throughout the body.	Range from fever, vomiting and loss of appetite in less severe cases to shock, irreversible kidney damage and possibly death in most severe cases.
Rabies	Potentially deadly virus that infects warm-blooded mammals.	Bite from a carrier of the virus, mainly wild animals.	1st stage: dog exhibits change in behavior, fear. 2nd stage: dog's behavior becomes more aggressive. 3rd stage: loss of coordination, trouble with bodily functions.
Parvovirus	Highly contagious virus, potentially deadly.	Ingestion of the virus, which is usually spread through the feces of infected dogs.	Most common: severe diarrhea. Also vomiting, fatigue, lack of appetite.
Canine cough	Contagious respiratory infection.	Combination of types of bacteria and virus. Most common: *Bordetella bronchiseptica* bacteria and parainfluenza virus.	Chronic cough.
Distemper	Disease primarily affecting respiratory and nervous system.	Virus that is related to the human measles virus.	Mild symptoms such as fever, lack of appetite and mucus secretion progress to evidence of brain damage, "hard pad."
Hepatitis	Virus primarily affecting the liver.	Canine adenovirus type I (CAV-1). Enters system when dog breathes in particles.	Lesser symptoms include listlessness, diarrhea, vomiting. More severe symptoms include "blue-eye" (clumps of virus in eye).
Coronavirus	Virus resulting in digestive problems.	Virus is spread through infected dog's feces.	Stomach upset evidenced by lack of appetite, vomiting, diarrhea.

pyometra in bitches and testicular cancer in males, it greatly reduces the risk of breast cancer in bitches and prostate cancer in male dogs.

Your vet should provide your puppy with a thorough dental evaluation at six months of age, ascertaining whether all of the permanent teeth have erupted properly. A home dental-care regimen should be initiated at six months, including brushing weekly and providing good dental devices (such as hard plastic or nylon bones). Regular dental care promotes healthy teeth, fresh breath and a longer life.

DOGS OLDER THAN ONE YEAR
Continue to visit the vet at least once a year. There is no such disease as "old age," but bodily functions do change with age. The eyes and ears are no longer as efficient. Liver, kidney and intestinal functions often decline. Proper dietary changes, recommended by your vet, can make life more pleasant for your aging Finnish Spitz and you.

SKIN PROBLEMS

Vets are consulted by dog owners for skin problems more than for any other group of diseases or maladies. A dog's skin is as sensitive, if not more so, than human skin, and both suffer from almost the same ailments (though the occurrence of acne in most dogs is rare). For this reason, veterinary dermatology has developed into a specialty practiced by many vets.

Since many skin problems have visual symptoms that are almost identical, it requires the skill of an experienced veterinary dermatologist to identify and cure many of the more severe skin disorders. Pet shops sell many treatments for skin problems, but most of the treatments are directed at symptoms and not at the underlying problem(s). If your dog is suffering from a skin disorder, you should seek professional assistance as quickly as possible. As with all diseases, the earlier a problem is identified and treated, the more likely it is that the cure will be successful.

HEREDITARY SKIN DISORDERS

Veterinary dermatologists are currently researching a number of skin disorders that are believed to have hereditary bases. These inherited diseases are transmitted by both parents, who appear (phenotypically) normal but have a recessive gene for the disease, meaning that they carry, but are not affected by, the disease. These diseases pose serious problems to breeders because in some instances there are no methods of identifying carriers. Often the secondary diseases associated with these skin conditions are even more debilitating than the skin disorders themselves, including cancers and respiratory problems.

Among the hereditary skin disorders for which the mode of inheritance is known are acrodermatitis, cutaneous asthenia (Ehlers-Danlos syndrome), sebaceous adenitis, cyclic hematopoiesis, dermatomyositis, IgA deficiency, color dilution alopecia and nodular dermatofibrosis. Some of these disorders are limited to one or two breeds, while others affect a large number of breeds. All inherited diseases must be diagnosed and treated by a veterinary specialist.

PARASITE BITES

Many of us are allergic to insect bites. The bites itch, erupt and may even become infected. Dogs have the same reaction to fleas, ticks and/or mites. When an insect lands on you, you have the chance to whisk it away with your hand. Unfortunately, when a dog is bitten by a flea, tick or mite, he can only scratch it away or bite it. By the time the dog has been bitten, the parasite has done some of its damage. It may

First Aid at a Glance

Burns
Place the affected area under cool water; use ice if only a small area is burnt.

Bee stings/Insect bites
Apply ice to relieve swelling; antihistamine dosed properly.

Animal bites
Clean any bleeding area; apply pressure until bleeding subsides; go to the vet.

Spider bites
Use cold compress and a pressurized pack to inhibit venom's spreading.

Antifreeze poisoning
Induce vomiting with hydrogen peroxide. Seek *immediate* veterinary help!

Fish hooks
Removal best handled by vet; hook must be cut in order to remove.

Snake bites
Pack ice around bite; contact vet quickly; identify snake for proper antivenin.

Car accident
Move dog from roadway with blanket; seek veterinary aid.

Shock
Calm the dog; keep him warm; seek immediate veterinary help.

Nosebleed
Apply cold compress to the nose; apply pressure to any visible abrasion.

Bleeding
Apply pressure above the area; treat wound by applying a cotton pack.

Heat stroke
Submerge dog in cold bath; cool down with fresh air and water; go to the vet.

Frostbite/Hypothermia
Warm the dog with a warm bath, electric blankets or hot water bottles.

Abrasions
Clean the wound and wash out thoroughly with fresh water; apply antiseptic.

 Remember: an injured dog may attempt to bite a helping hand from fear and confusion. Always muzzle the dog before trying to offer assistance.

also have laid eggs, which will cause further problems in the near future. The itching from parasite bites is probably due to the saliva injected into the site when the parasite sucks the dog's blood.

AIRBORNE ALLERGIES

Just as humans suffer from hay fever during the pollinating season, many dogs suffer from the same allergies. When the pollen count is high, your dog might suffer, but don't expect him to sneeze and have a runny nose as a human would. Dogs react to pollen allergies in the same way they react to fleas— they scratch and bite themselves. Dogs, like humans, can be tested for allergens. Discuss the testing with your vet.

VITAL SIGNS

A dog's normal temperature is 101.5 degrees Fahrenheit. A range of between 100.0 and 102.5 degrees should be considered normal, as each dog's body sets its own temperature. It will be helpful if you take your dog's temperature when you know he is healthy and record it. Then, when you suspect that he is not feeling well, you will have a normal figure to compare the abnormal temperature against.

The normal pulse rate for a dog is between 100 and 125 beats per minute.

AUTO-IMMUNE ILLNESSES

An auto-immune illness is one in which the immune system over-acts and does not recognize parts of the affected person; rather, the immune system starts to react as if these parts were foreign and need to be destroyed. An example is rheumatoid arthritis, which occurs when the body does not recognize the joints, thus leading to a very painful and damaging reaction in the joints. This has nothing to do with age, so can occur in children and young dogs. The wear-and-tear arthritis of the older person or dog is osteoarthritis.

Lupus is an auto-immune disease that affects dogs as well as people. It can take variable forms, affecting the kidneys, bones and the skin. It can be fatal, so is treated with steroids, which can themselves have very significant side effects. The steroids calm down the allergic reaction to the body's tissues, which helps the lupus; however, the steroids also decrease the body's reaction to real foreign substances such as bacteria, and they also thin the skin and bone.

FOOD PROBLEMS

FOOD ALLERGIES

Some dogs can be allergic to many foods that may be best-sellers and highly recommended by breeders and vets. Changing

THE PROTEIN QUESTION
Your dog's protein needs are change-able. High activity level, stress, climate and other physical factors may require your dog to have more protein in his diet. Check with your veterinarian.

the brand of food that you buy may not eliminate the problem if the element to which the dog is allergic is contained in the new brand.

Recognizing a food allergy in a dog can be difficult. Humans often have rashes when we eat foods to which we are allergic, or have swelling of the lips or eyes. Dogs do not usually develop rashes, but react in the same way as they do to an airborne or bite allergy—they itch, scratch and bite. While pollen allergies are usually seasonal, food allergies are year-round problems.

TREATING FOOD ALLERGY
Diagnosis of food allergy is based on a two- to four-week dietary trial with a home-cooked diet fed to the exclusion of all other foods. The diet should consist of boiled rice or potato with a source of protein that the dog has never eaten before. Beef and chicken are common in dogs' diets, so try something like fresh or frozen fish, lamb or even something as exotic as pheasant. Water has to be the only drink, and it is really important that no other foods are fed during this trial.

If the dog's condition improves, you will need to try the original diet once again to see if the itching resumes. If it does, then this confirms the diagnosis that the dog is allergic to his orig-inal diet. The treatment is long-term feeding of something that does not distress the dog's skin, which may be in the form of one of the commercially available hypoallergenic diets or the home-made diet that you created for the allergy trial.

FOOD INTOLERANCE
Food intolerance is the inability of the dog to completely digest certain foods. This occurs because the dog does not have the chemicals necessary to digest some foodstuffs. These chemicals are called enzymes. All puppies have the enzymes necessary to digest canine milk, but some dogs do not have the enzymes to digest a very different form of milk that is commonly found in human households—milk from cows. In such dogs, drinking cows' milk results in loose bowels, stomach pains and the passage of gas. Dogs often also do not have the enzymes to digest soy or other beans. The treatment for food intolerance is to exclude the foodstuffs that upset your Finnish Spitz's digestion.

A male dog flea, *Ctenocephalides canis*.

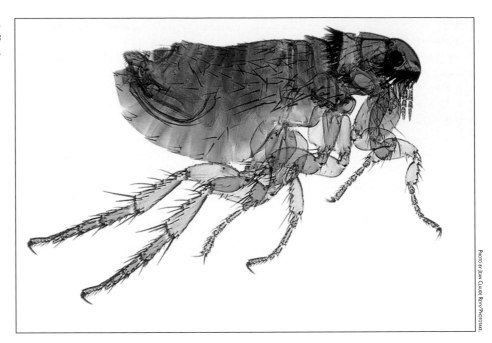

PHOTO BY JEAN CLAUDE REVY/PHOTOTAKE

EXTERNAL PARASITES

FLEAS

Of all the problems to which dogs are prone, none is more well known and frustrating than fleas. Flea infestation is relatively simple to cure but difficult to prevent. Parasites that are harbored inside the body are a bit more difficult to eradicate but they are easier to control.

To control flea infestation, you have to understand the flea's life cycle. Fleas are often thought of as a summertime problem, but centrally heated homes have changed the patterns and fleas can be found at any time of the year. The most effective method of flea control is a two-stage approach: one stage to kill the adult fleas, and the other to control the development of pre-adult fleas. Unfortunately, no single active ingredient is effective against all stages of the life cycle.

FLEA KILLER CAUTION— "POISON"

Flea-killers are poisonous. You should not spray these toxic chemicals on areas of a dog's body that he licks, including his genitals and his face. Flea killers taken internally are a better answer, but check with your vet in case internal therapy is not advised for your dog.

LIFE CYCLE STAGES

During its life, a flea will pass through four life stages: egg, larva, pupa or nymph and adult. The adult stage is the most visible and irritating stage of the flea life cycle, and this is why the majority of flea-control products concentrate on this stage. The fact is that adult fleas account for only 1% of the total flea population, and the other 99% exist in pre-adult stages, i.e., eggs, larvae and nymphs. The pre-adult stages are barely visible to the naked eye.

THE LIFE CYCLE OF THE FLEA

Eggs are laid on the dog, usually in quantities of about 20 or 30, several times a day. The adult female flea must have a blood meal before each egg-laying session. When first laid, the eggs will cling to the dog's hair, as the eggs are still moist. However, they will quickly dry out and fall from the dog, especially if the dog moves around or scratches. Many eggs will fall off in the dog's favorite area or an area in which he spends a lot of time, such as his bed.

Once the eggs fall from the dog onto the carpet or furniture, they will hatch into larvae. This takes from one to ten days. Larvae are not particularly mobile and will usually travel only a few inches from where they hatch. However, they do have a tendency to move away from

EN GARDE:
CATCHING FLEAS OFF GUARD!
Consider the following ways to arm yourself against fleas:
- Add a small amount of pennyroyal or eucalyptus oil to your dog's bath. These natural remedies repel fleas.
- Supplement your dog's food with fresh garlic (minced or grated) and a hearty amount of brewer's yeast, both of which ward off fleas.
- Use a flea comb on your dog daily. Submerge fleas in a cup of bleach to kill them quickly.
- Confine the dog to only a few rooms to limit the spread of fleas in the home.
- Vacuum daily...and get all of the crevices! Dispose of the bag every few days until the problem is under control.
- Wash your dog's bedding daily. Cover cushions where your dog sleeps with towels, and wash the towels often.

bright light and heavy traffic—under furniture and behind doors are common places to find high quantities of flea larvae.

The flea larvae feed on dead organic matter, including adult flea feces, until they are ready to change into adult fleas. Fleas will usually remain as larvae for around seven days. After this period, the larvae will pupate into protective pupae. While inside the pupae, the larvae will undergo metamorphosis and change into adult fleas. This can take as little time as a few days, but the adult fleas can remain inside the pupae waiting to hatch for up to two years. The pupae are signaled to hatch by certain stimuli, such as physical pressure—the pupae's being stepped on, heat from an animal's lying on the pupae or increased carbon-dioxide levels and vibrations—indicating that a suitable host is available.

Once hatched, the adult flea must feed within a few days. Once the adult flea finds a host, it will not leave voluntarily. It only becomes dislodged by grooming

PHOTO BY DWIGHT R. KUHN.

or the host animal's scratching. The adult flea will remain on the host for the duration of its life unless forcibly removed.

TREATING THE ENVIRONMENT AND THE DOG

Treating fleas should be a two-pronged attack. First, the environment needs to be treated; this includes carpets and furniture, especially the dog's bedding and areas underneath furniture. The environment should be treated with a household spray containing an Insect Growth Regulator (IGR) and an insecticide to kill the adult fleas. Most IGRs are effective against eggs and larvae; they actually mimic the fleas' own hormones and stop the eggs and larvae from developing into adult fleas. There are currently no treatments available to attack the pupa stage of the life cycle, so the adult insecticide is used to kill the newly hatched adult fleas before they find a host. Most IGRs are active for many months, while

S. E. M. BY DR DENNIS KUNKEL, UNIVERSITY OF HAWAII.

THE LIFE CYCLE OF THE FLEA

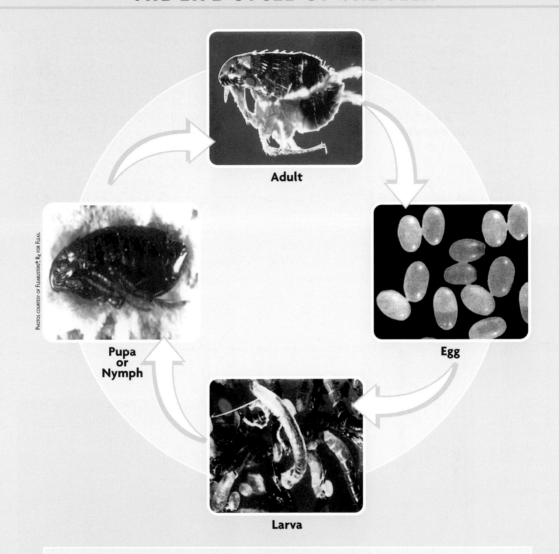

Adult

Egg

Larva

**Pupa
or
Nymph**

Fleas have been around for millions of years and have adapted to changing host animals. They are able to go through a complete life cycle in less than one month or they can extend their lives to almost two years by remaining as pupae or cocoons. They do not need blood or any other food for up to 20 months.

Two types of products should be used when treating fleas—a product to treat the pet and a product to treat the home. Adult fleas represent less than 1% of the flea population. The pre-adult fleas (eggs, larvae and pupae) represent more than 99% of the flea population and are found in the environment; it is in the case of pre-adult fleas that products containing an Insect Growth Regulator (IGR) should be used in the home.

IGRs are a new class of compounds used to prevent the development of insects. They do not kill the insect outright, but instead use the insect's biology against it to stop it from completing its growth. Products that contain methoprene are the world's first and leading IGRs. Used to control fleas and other insects, this type of IGR will stop flea larvae from developing and protect the house for up to seven months.

The American dog tick, *Dermacentor variabilis*, is probably the most common tick found on dogs. Look at the strength in its eight legs! No wonder it's hard to detach them.

adult insecticides are only active for a few days.

When treating with a house-hold spray, it is a good idea to vacuum before applying the product. This stimulates as many pupae as possible to hatch into adult fleas. The vacuum cleaner should also be treated with an insecticide to prevent the eggs and larvae that have been collected in the vacuum bag from hatching.

The second stage of treatment is to apply an adult insecticide to the dog. Traditionally, this would be in the form of a collar or a spray, but more recent innovations include digestible insecticides that poison the fleas when they ingest the dog's blood. Alternatively, there are drops that, when placed on the back of the dog's neck, spread throughout the hair and skin to kill adult fleas.

TICKS

Though not as common as fleas, ticks are found all over the tropical and temperate world. They don't bite, like fleas; they harpoon. They dig their sharp proboscis (nose) into the dog's skin and drink the blood. Their

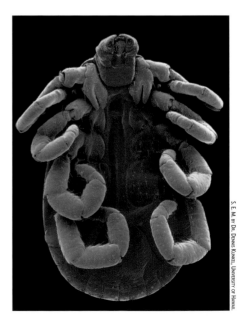

only food and drink is dog's blood. Dogs can get Lyme disease, Rocky Mountain spotted fever, tick bite paralysis and many other diseases from ticks. They may live where fleas are found and they like to hide in cracks or seams in walls. They are controlled the same way fleas are controlled.

The American dog tick, *Dermacentor variabilis*, may well be the most common dog tick in many geographical areas, especially those areas where the climate is hot and humid. Most dog ticks have life expectancies of a week to six months, depending upon climatic conditions. They can neither jump nor fly, but they can crawl slowly and can range up to 16 feet to reach a sleeping or unsuspecting dog.

MITES

Just as fleas and ticks can be problematic for your dog, mites can also lead to an itchy nuisance. Microscopic in size, mites are related to ticks and generally take up permanent residence on their host animal—in this case, your dog! The term *mange* refers to any infestation caused by one of the mighty mites, of which there are six varieties that concern dog owners.

Demodex mites cause a condition known as demodicosis (sometimes called red mange or follicular mange), in which the

DEER-TICK CROSSING

The great outdoors may be fun for your dog, but it also is a home to dangerous ticks. Deer ticks carry a bacterium known as *Borrelia burgdorferi* and are most active in the autumn and spring. When infections are caught early, penicillin and tetracycline are effective antibiotics, but, if left untreated, the bacteria may cause neurological, kidney and cardiac problems as well as long-term trouble with walking and painful joints.

S.E.M. BY DR. ANDREW SPIELMAN/PHOTOTAKE.

PHOTO BY DR. DENNIS KUNKEL, UNIVERSITY OF HAWAII.

The head of an American dog tick, *Dermacentor variabilis*, enlarged and colorized for effect.

The mange mite, *Psoroptes bovis*, can infest cattle and other domestic animals.

PHOTO BY JAMES HAYDEN/YOAV/PHOTOTAKE.

Human lice look like dog lice; the two are closely related.

PHOTO BY DWIGHT R. KUHN.

mites live in the dog's hair follicles and sebaceous glands in larger-than-normal numbers. This type of mange is commonly passed from the dam to her puppies and usually shows up on the puppies' muzzles, though demodicosis is not transferable from one normal dog to another. Most dogs recover from this type of mange without any treatment, though topical therapies are commonly prescribed by the vet.

The *Cheyletiellosis* mite is the hook-mouthed culprit associated with "walking dandruff," a condi-

tion that affects dogs as well as cats and rabbits. This mite lives on the surface of the animal's skin and is readily transferable through direct or indirect contact with an affected animal. The dandruff is present in the form of scaly skin, which may or may not be itchy. If not treated, this mange can affect a whole kennel of dogs and can be spread to humans as well.

The *Sarcoptes* mite causes intense itching on the dog in the form of a condition known as scabies or sarcoptic mange. The cycle of the *Sarcoptes* mite lasts about three weeks, and the mites live in the top layer of the dog's skin (epidermis), preferably in areas with little hair. Scabies is highly contagious and can be passed to humans. Sometimes an allergic reaction to the mite worsens the severe itching associated with sarcoptic mange.

Ear mites, *Otodectes cynotis,* lead to otodectic mange, which most commonly affects the outer ear canal of the dog, though other areas can be affected as well. Dogs with ear-mite infestation commonly scratch at their ears, causing further irritation, and shake their heads. Dark brown droppings in the outer ear confirm the diagnosis. Your vet can prescribe a treatment to flush out the ears and kill any eggs in the ears. A complete month of treatment is necessary to cure the mange.

Two other mites, less common in dogs, include *Dermanyssus gallinae* (the poultry or red mite) and *Eutrombicula alfreddugesi* (the North American mite associated with trombiculidiasis or chigger infestation). The poultry mite frequently lives on chickens, but can transfer to dogs who spend time near farm animals. Chigger infestation affects dogs in

DO NOT MIX

Never mix parasite-control products without first consulting your vet. Some products can become toxic when combined with others and can cause fatal consequences.

NOT A DROP TO DRINK

Never allow your dog to swim in polluted water or public areas where water quality can be suspect. Even perfectly clear water can harbor parasites, many of which can cause serious to fatal illnesses in canines. Areas inhabited by waterfowl and other wildlife are especially dangerous.

the Central US who have exposure to woodlands. The types of mange caused by both of these mites are treatable by vets.

INTERNAL PARASITES

Most animals—fishes, birds and mammals, including dogs and humans—have worms and other parasites that live inside their bodies. According to Dr. Herbert R. Axelrod, the fish pathologist, there are two kinds of parasites: dumb and smart. The smart parasites live in peaceful cooperation with their hosts (symbiosis), while the dumb parasites kill their hosts. Most worm infections are relatively easy to control. If they are not controlled, they weaken the host dog to the point that other medical problems occur, but they do not kill the host as dumb parasites would.

A brown dog tick, *Rhipicephalus sanguineus,* is an uncommon but annoying tick found on dogs.

PHOTO BY CAROLINA BIOLOGICAL SUPPLY/PHOTOTAKE

The roundworm *Rhabditis* can infect both dogs and humans.

ROUNDWORMS

Average-size dogs can pass 1,360,000 roundworm eggs every day. For example, if there were only 1 million dogs in the world, the world would be saturated with thousands of tons of dog feces. These feces would contain around 15,000,000,000 roundworm eggs.

Up to 31% of home yards and children's sand boxes in the US contain roundworm eggs.

Flushing dog's feces down the toilet is not a safe practice because the usual sewage treatments do not destroy roundworm eggs.

Infected puppies start shedding roundworm eggs at three weeks of age. They can be infected by their mother's milk.

The roundworm, *Ascaris lumbricoides.*

PHOTO BY DWIGHT R. KUHN

ROUNDWORMS

The roundworms that infect dogs are known scientifically as *Toxocara canis.* They live in the dog's intestines and shed eggs continually. It has been estimated that a dog produces about 6 or more ounces of feces every day. Each ounce of feces averages hundreds of thousands of roundworm eggs. There are no known areas in which dogs roam that do not contain roundworm eggs. The greatest danger of roundworms is that they infect people, too! It is wise to have your dog tested regularly for roundworms.

In young puppies, roundworms cause bloated bellies, diarrhea, coughing and vomiting, and are transmitted from the dam (through blood or milk). Affected puppies will not appear as animated as normal puppies. The worms appear spaghetti-like, measuring as long as 6 inches. Adult dogs can acquire roundworms through coprophagia (eating contaminated feces) or by killing rodents that carry roundworms.

Roundworm infection can kill puppies and cause severe problems in adults, as the hatched larvae travel to the lungs and trachea through the bloodstream. Cleanliness is the best preventative for roundworms. Always pick up after your dog and dispose of feces in appropriate receptacles.

PHOTO BY DWIGHT R. KUHN.

HOOKWORMS

In the United States, dog owners have to be concerned about four different species of hookworm, the most common and most serious of which is *Ancylostoma caninum,* which prefers warm climates. The others are *Ancylostoma braziliense, Ancylostoma tubaeforme* and *Uncinaria stenocephala,* the latter of which is a concern to dogs living in the Northern US and Canada, as this species prefers cold climates. Hookworms are dangerous to humans as well as to dogs and cats, and can be the cause of severe anemia due to iron deficiency. The worm uses its teeth to attach itself to the dog's intestines and changes the site of its attachment about six times per day. Each time the

worm repositions itself, the dog loses blood and can become anemic. *Ancylostoma caninum* is the most likely of the four species to cause anemia in the dog.

Symptoms of hookworm infection include dark stools, weight loss, general weakness, pale coloration and anemia, as well as possible skin problems. Fortunately, hookworms are easily purged from the affected dog with a number of medications that have proven effective. Discuss these with your vet. Most heartworm preventatives include a hookworm insecticide as well.

Owners also must be aware that hookworms can infect humans, who can acquire the larvae through exposure to contaminated feces. Since the worms cannot complete their life cycle on a human, the worms simply infest the skin and cause irritation. This condition is known as cutaneous larva migrans syndrome. As a preventative, use disposable gloves or a "poop-scoop" to pick up your dog's droppings and prevent your dog (or neighborhood cats) from defecating in children's play areas.

The hookworm, *Ancylostoma caninum.*

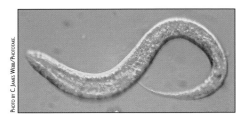

PHOTO BY C. JAMES WEBB/PHOTOTAKE.

The infective stage of the hookworm larva.

TAPEWORMS

Humans, rats, squirrels, foxes, coyotes, wolves and domestic dogs are all susceptible to tapeworm infection. Except in humans, tapeworms are usually not a fatal infection. Infected individuals can harbor 1000 parasitic worms.

Tapeworms, like some other types of worm, are hermaphroditic, meaning male and female in the same worm.

If dogs eat infected rats or mice, or anything else infected with tapeworm, they get the tapeworm disease. One month after attaching to a dog's intestine, the worm starts shedding eggs. These eggs are infective immediately. Infective eggs can live for a few months without a host animal.

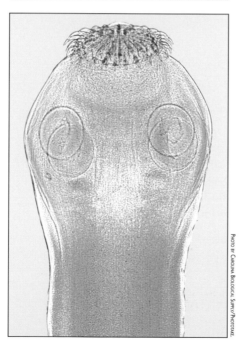

The head and rostellum (the round prominence on the scolex) of a tapeworm, which infects dogs and humans.

PHOTO BY CAROLINA BIOLOGICAL SUPPLY/PHOTOTAKE

TAPEWORMS

There are many species of tapeworm, all of which are carried by fleas! The most common tapeworm affecting dogs is known as *Dipylidium caninum*. The dog eats the flea and starts the tapeworm cycle. Humans can also be infected with tapeworms—so don't eat fleas! Fleas are so small that your dog could pass them onto your hands, your plate or your food and thus make it possible for you to ingest a flea that is carrying tapeworm eggs.

While tapeworm infection is not life-threatening in dogs (smart parasite!), it can be the cause of a very serious liver disease for humans. About 50% of the humans infected with *Echinococcus multilocularis*, a type of tapeworm that causes alveolar hydatid, perish.

WHIPWORMS

In North America, whipworms are counted among the most common parasitic worms in dogs. The whipworm's scientific name is *Trichuris vulpis*. These worms attach themselves in the lower parts of the intestine, where they feed. Affected dogs may only experience upset tummies, colic and diarrhea. These worms, however, can live for months or years in the dog, beginning their larval stage in the small intestine, spending their adult stage in the large intestine and finally passing infective eggs through the dog's feet. The only way to detect whipworms is through a fecal examination, though this is not always foolproof. Treatment for whipworms is tricky, due to the worms' unusual life-cycle pattern, and very often dogs are reinfected due to exposure to infective eggs on the ground. The whipworm eggs can survive in the environment for as long as five years; thus, cleaning up droppings in your own backyard as well as in public places is absolutely essential for sanitation purposes and the health of your dog and others.

THREADWORMS

Though less common than round-worms, hookworms and those previously mentioned, thread-worms concern dog owners in the Southwestern US and Gulf Coast area where the climate is hot and humid. Living in the small intestine of the dog, this worm measures a mere 2 millimeters and is round in shape. Like that of the whipworm, the threadworm's life cycle is very complex and the eggs and larvae are passed through the feces. A deadly disease in humans, *Strongyloides* readily infects people, and the handling of feces is the most common means of transmission. Threadworms are most often seen in young puppies; bloody diarrhea and pneumonia are symptoms. Sick puppies must be isolated and treated immediately; vets recommend a follow-up treatment one month later.

HEARTWORM PREVENTATIVES

There are many heartworm preventatives on the market, many of which are sold at your veterinarian's office. These products can be given daily or monthly, depending on the manufacturer's instructions. All of these preventatives contain chemical insecticides directed at killing heartworms, which leads to some controversy among dog owners. In effect, heartworm preventatives are necessary evils, though you should determine how necessary based on your pet's lifestyle. There is no doubt that heartworm is a dreadful disease that threatens the lives of dogs. However, the likelihood of your dog's being bitten by an infected mosquito is slim in most places, and a mosquito-repellent (or an herbal remedy such as Wormwood or Black Walnut) is much safer for your dog and will not compromise his immune system (the way heartworm preventatives will). Should you decide to use the traditional preventative "medications," you can consider giving the pill every other or third month. Since the toxins in the pill will kill the heartworms at all stages of development, the pill would be effective in killing larvae, nymphs or adults, and it takes four months for the larvae to reach the adult stage. Thus, there is no rationale to poisoning the dog's system on a monthly basis. Lastly, do not give the pill during the winter months, since there are no mosquitoes around to pass on their infection, unless you live in a tropical environment.

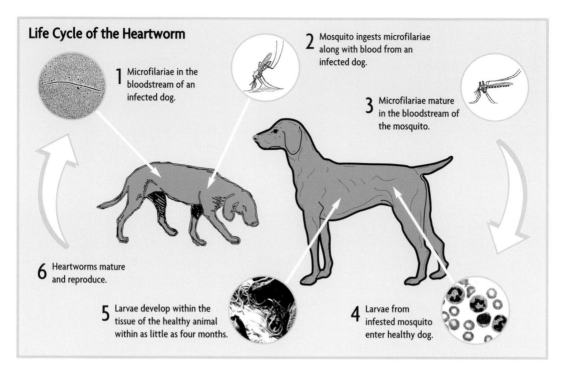

Life Cycle of the Heartworm

1 Microfilariae in the bloodstream of an infected dog.

2 Mosquito ingests microfilariae along with blood from an infected dog.

3 Microfilariae mature in the bloodstream of the mosquito.

4 Larvae from infested mosquito enter healthy dog.

5 Larvae develop within the tissue of the healthy animal within as little as four months.

6 Heartworms mature and reproduce.

HEARTWORMS

Heartworms are thin, extended worms up to 12 inches long, which live in a dog's heart and the major blood vessels surrounding it. Dogs may have up to 200 worms. Symptoms may be loss of energy, loss of appetite, coughing, the development of a pot belly and anemia.

Heartworms are transmitted by mosquitoes. The mosquito drinks the blood of an infected dog and takes in larvae with the blood. The larvae, called microfilariae, develop within the body of the mosquito and are passed on to the next dog bitten after the larvae mature. It takes two to three weeks for the larvae to develop to the infective stage within the body of the mosquito. Dogs are usually treated at about six weeks of age and maintained on a prophylactic dose given monthly.

Blood testing for heartworms is not necessarily indicative of how seriously your dog is infected. Although this is a dangerous disease, it is not easy for a dog to be infected. Discuss the various preventatives with your vet, as there are many different types now available. Together you can decide on a safe course of prevention for your dog.

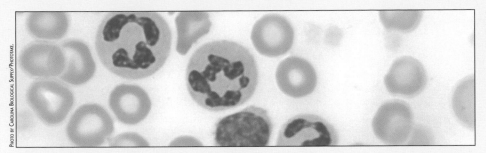

Magnified heart-worm larvae, *Dirofilaria immitis.*

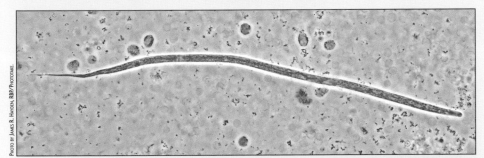

Heartworm, *Dirofilaria immitis.*

The heart of a dog infected with canine heart-worm, *Dirofilaria immitis.*

HOMEOPATHY:
an alternative to conventional medicine

"Less is Most"

Using this principle, the strength of a homeopathic remedy is measured by the number of serial dilutions that were undertaken to create it. The greater the number of serial dilutions, the greater the strength of the homeopathic remedy. The potency of a remedy that has been made by making a dilution of 1 part in 100 parts (or 1/100) is 1c or 1cH. If this remedy is subjected to a series of further dilutions, each one being 1/100, a more dilute and stronger remedy is produced. If the remedy is diluted in this way six times, it is called 6c or 6cH. A dilution of 6c is 1 part in 1,000,000,000,000. In general, higher potencies in more frequent doses are better for acute symptoms and lower potencies in more infrequent doses are more useful for chronic, long-standing problems.

CURING OUR DOGS NATURALLY

Holistic medicine means treating the whole animal as a unique, perfect, living being. Generally, holistic treatments do not suppress the symptoms that the body naturally produces, as do most medications prescribed by conventional doctors and vets. Holistic methods seek to cure disease by regaining balance and harmony in the patient's environment. Some of these methods include use of nutritional therapy, herbs, flower essences, aromatherapy, acupuncture, massage, chiropractic and, of course, the most popular holistic approach, homeopathy.

Homeopathy is a theory or system of treating illness with small doses of substances which, if administered in larger quantities, would produce the symptoms that the patient already has. This approach is often described as "like cures like." Although modern veterinary medicine is geared toward the "quick fix," homeopathy relies on the belief that, given the time, the body is able to heal itself and return to its natural, healthy state.

Choosing a remedy to cure a problem in our dogs is the difficult part of homeopathy. Consult with your vet for a professional diagnosis of your dog's symptoms. Often these symptoms require immediate conventional care. If your vet is willing and knowledgeable, you may attempt a homeopathic remedy. Be aware that cortisone prevents homeopathic remedies from working. There are hundreds of possibilities and combinations to cure many problems in dogs, from basic physical problems such as excessive shedding, fleas or other parasites, unattractive doggy odor, bad breath, upset tummy, obesity, dry, oily or dull coat, diarrhea, ear problems or eye discharge (including tears and dry or mucousy matter), to behavioral abnormalities such as fear of loud noises, habitual licking, poor appetite, excessive barking and various phobias. From alumina to zincum metallicum, the remedies span the planet and the imagination…from flowers and weeds to chemicals, insect droppings, diesel smoke and volcanic ash.

Using "Like to Treat Like"

Unlike conventional medicines that suppress symptoms, homeopathic remedies treat illnesses with small doses of substances that, if administered in larger quantities, would produce the symptoms that the patient already has. While the same homeopathic remedy can be used to treat different symptoms in different dogs, here are some interesting remedies and their uses.

Apis Mellifica
(made from honey bee venom) can be used for allergies or to reduce swelling that occurs in acutely infected kidneys.

Diesel Smoke
can be used to help control travel sickness.

Calcarea Fluorica
(made from calcium fluoride, which helps harden bone structure) can be useful in treating hard lumps in tissues.

Natrum Muriaticum
(made from common salt, sodium chloride) is useful in treating thin, thirsty dogs.

Nitricum Acidum
(made from nitric acid) is used for symptoms you would expect to see from contact with acids, such as lesions, especially where the skin joins the linings of body orifices or openings such as the lips and nostrils.

Symphytum
(made from the herb Knitbone, *Symphytum officianale*) is used to encourage bones to heal.

Urtica Urens
(made from the common stinging nettle) is used in treating painful, irritating rashes.

HOMEOPATHIC REMEDIES FOR YOUR DOG

Symptom/Ailment	Possible Remedy
ALLERGIES	Apis Mellifica 30c, Astacus Fluviatilis 6c, Pulsatilla 30c, Urtica Urens 6c
ALOPECIA	Alumina 30c, Lycopodium 30c, Sepia 30c, Thallium 6c
ANAL GLANDS (BLOCKED)	Hepar Sulphuris Calcareum 30c, Sanicula 6c, Silicea 6c
ARTHRITIS	Rhus Toxicodendron 6c, Bryonia Alba 6c
CANINE COUGH	Drosera 6c, Ipecacuanha 30c
CATARACT	Calcarea Carbonica 6c, Conium Maculatum 6c, Phosphorus 30c, Silicea 30c
CONSTIPATION	Alumina 6c, Carbo Vegetabilis 30c, Graphites 6c, Nitricum Acidum 30c, Silicea 6c
COUGHING	Aconitum Napellus 6c, Belladonna 30c, Hyoscyamus Niger 30c, Phosphorus 30c
DIARRHEA	Arsenicum Album 30c, Aconitum Napellus 6c, Chamomilla 30c, Mercurius Corrosivus 30c
DRY EYE	Zincum Metallicum 30c
EAR PROBLEMS	Aconitum Napellus 30c, Belladonna 30c, Hepar Sulphuris 30c, Tellurium 30c, Psorinum 200c
EYE PROBLEMS	Borax 6c, Aconitum Napellus 30c, Graphites 6c, Staphysagria 6c, Thuja Occidentalis 30c
GLAUCOMA	Aconitum Napellus 30c, Apis Mellifica 6c, Phosphorus 30c
HEAT STROKE	Belladonna 30c, Gelsemium Sempervirens 30c, Sulphur 30c
HICCOUGHS	Cinchona Deficinalis 6c
HIP DYSPLASIA	Colocynthis 6c, Rhus Toxicodendron 6c, Bryonia Alba 6c
INCONTINENCE	Argentum Nitricum 6c, Causticum 30c, Conium Maculatum 30c, Pulsatilla 30c, Sepia 30c
INSECT BITES	Apis Mellifica 30c, Cantharis 30c, Hypericum Perforatum 6c, Urtica Urens 30c
ITCHING	Alumina 30c, Arsenicum Album 30c, Carbo Vegetabilis 30c, Hypericum Perforatum 6c, Mezerium 6c, Sulphur 30c
MASTITIS	Apis Mellifica 30c, Belladonna 30c, Urtica Urens 1m
MOTION SICKNESS	Cocculus 6c, Petroleum 6c
PATELLAR LUXATION	Gelsemium Sempervirens 6c, Rhus Toxicodendron 6c
PENIS PROBLEMS	Aconitum Napellus 30c, Hepar Sulphuris Calcareum 30c, Pulsatilla 30c, Thuja Occidentalis 6c
PUPPY TEETHING	Calcarea Carbonica 6c, Chamomilla 6c, Phytolacca 6c

Recognizing a Sick Dog

Unlike colicky babies and cranky children, our canine kids cannot tell us when they are feeling ill. Therefore, there are a number of signs that owners can identify to know that their dogs are not feeling well.

Take note for physical manifestations such as:

- unusual, bad odor, including bad breath
- excessive shedding
- wax in the ears, chronic ear irritation
- oily, flaky, dull haircoat
- mucus, tearing or similar discharge in the eyes
- fleas or mites
- mucus in stool, diarrhea
- sensitivity to petting or handling
- licking at paws, scratching face, etc.

Keep an eye out for behavioral changes as well including:

- lethargy, idleness
- lack of patience or general irritability
- lack of interest in food
- phobias (fear of people, loud noises, etc.)
- strange behavior, suspicion, fear
- coprophagia
- more frequent barking
- whimpering, crying

Get Well Soon

You don't need a DVM to provide good TLC to your sick or recovering dog, but you do need to pay attention to some details that normally wouldn't bother him. The following tips will aid Fido's recovery and get him back on his paws again:

- Keep his space free of irritating smells, like heavy perfumes and air fresheners.
- Rest is the best medicine! Avoid harsh lighting that will prevent your dog from sleeping. Shade him from bright sunlight during the day and dim the lights in the evening.
- Keep the noise level down. Animals are more sensitive to sound when they are sick.

- Be attentive to any necessary temperature adjustments. A dog with a fever needs a cool room and cold liquids. A bitch that is whelping or recovering from surgery will be more comfortable in a warm room, consuming warm liquids and food.
- You wouldn't send a sick child back to school early, so don't rush your dog back into a full routine until he seems absolutely ready.

Number-One Killer Disease in Dogs: CANCER

In every age, there is a word associated with a disease or plague that causes humans to shudder. In the 21st century, that word is "cancer." Just as cancer is the leading cause of death in humans, it claims nearly half the lives of dogs that die from a natural disease as well as half the dogs that die over the age of ten years.

Described as a genetic disease, cancer becomes a greater risk as the dog ages. Vets and dog owners have become increasingly aware of the threat of cancer to dogs. Statistics reveal that one dog in every five will develop cancer, the most common of which is skin cancer. Many cancers, including prostate, ovarian and breast cancer, can be avoided by spaying and neutering our dogs by the age of six months.

Early detection of cancer can save or extend a dog's life, so it is absolutely vital for owners to have their dogs examined by a qualified vet or oncologist immediately upon detection of any abnormality. Certain dietary guidelines have also proven to reduce the onset and spread of cancer. Foods based on fish rather than beef, due to the presence of Omega-3 fatty acids, are recommended. Other amino acids such as glutamine have significant benefits for canines, particularly those breeds that show a greater susceptibility to cancer.

Cancer management and treatments promise hope for future generations of canines. Since the disease is genetic, breeders should never breed a dog whose parents, grandparents and any related siblings have developed cancer. It is difficult to know whether to exclude an otherwise healthy dog from a breeding program, as the disease does not manifest itself until the dog's senior years.

RECOGNIZE CANCER WARNING SIGNS

Since early detection can possibly rescue your dog from becoming a cancer statistic, it is essential for owners to recognize the possible signs and seek the assistance of a qualified professional.

- Abnormal bumps or lumps that continue to grow
- Bleeding or discharge from any body cavity
- Persistent stiffness or lameness
- Recurrent sores or sores that do not heal
- Inappetence
- Breathing difficulties
- Weight loss
- Bad breath or odors
- General malaise and fatigue
- Eating and swallowing problems
- Difficulty urinating and defecating

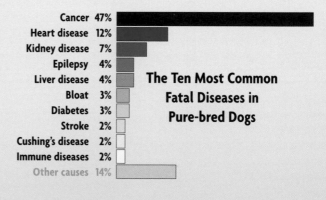

Disease	%
Cancer	47%
Heart disease	12%
Kidney disease	7%
Epilepsy	4%
Liver disease	4%
Bloat	3%
Diabetes	3%
Stroke	2%
Cushing's disease	2%
Immune diseases	2%
Other causes	14%

The Ten Most Common Fatal Diseases in Pure-bred Dogs

CDS: COGNITIVE DYSFUNCTION SYNDROME
"Old-Dog Syndrome"

There are many ways for you to evaluate old-dog syndrome. Veterinarians have defined CDS (cognitive dysfunction syndrome) as the gradual deterioration of cognitive abilities. These are indicated by changes in the dog's behavior. When a dog changes his routine response, and maladies have been eliminated as the cause of these behavioral changes, then CDS is the usual diagnosis.

More than half the dogs over eight years old suffer from some form of CDS. The older the dog, the more chance he has of suffering from CDS. In humans, doctors often dismiss the CDS behavioral changes as part of "winding down."

There are four major signs of CDS: frequent potty accidents inside the home, sleeping much more or much less than normal, acting confused and failing to respond to social stimuli.

SYMPTOMS OF CDS

FREQUENT POTTY ACCIDENTS
- *Urinates in the house.*
- *Defecates in the house.*
- *Doesn't signal that he wants to go out.*

SLEEP PATTERNS
- *Moves much more slowly.*
- *Sleeps more than normal during the day.*
- *Sleeps less during the night.*

CONFUSION
- *Goes outside and just stands there.*
- *Appears confused with a faraway look in his eyes.*
- *Hides more often.*
- *Doesn't recognize friends.*
- *Doesn't come when called.*
- *Walks around listlessly and without a destination.*

FAILURE TO RESPOND TO SOCIAL STIMULI
- *Comes to people less frequently, whether called or not.*
- *Doesn't tolerate petting for more than a short time.*
- *Doesn't come to the door when you return home.*

The term "old" is a qualitative term. For dogs, as well as for their masters, old is relative. Certainly we can all distinguish between a puppy Finnish Spitz and an adult Finnish Spitz—there are the obvious physical traits, such as size, appearance and facial expressions, along with the personality traits. Puppies and young dogs like to play with children. Children's natural exuberance is a good match for the seemingly endless energy of young dogs. They like to run, jump, chase and retrieve. When dogs grow older and cease their interaction with children, they are often thought of as being too old to keep pace with the children. On the other hand, if a Finnish Spitz is only exposed to people with quieter lifestyles, his life will normally be less active and the decrease in his activity level as he ages will not be as obvious.

If people live to be 100 years old, dogs live to be 20 years old. While this might seem like a good rule of thumb, it is very inaccurate. When trying to compare dog years to human years, you cannot make a generalization about all dogs. You can make the general-

ization that 12 to 13 years is the average lifespan for a Finnish Spitz, but members of the breed reaching the age of 15 is not unusual at all.

Dogs generally are considered physically mature at three years of age (or earlier), but can reproduce even earlier. So the first three years of a dog's life are like seven times that of comparable humans. That means a 3-year-old dog is like a 21-year-old human. However, the Finnish Spitz throws off this curve of comparison, as they take closer to four years to reach adulthood. As you can see, there is no hard and fast rule for comparing dog and human ages. Other factors to consider are that small breeds tend to live longer than large breeds, some breeds' adolescent periods last longer than others' and some breeds experience rapid periods of growth. The comparison is made even more difficult, for, likewise, not all humans age at the same rate!

WHAT TO LOOK FOR IN SENIORS
Most vets and behaviorists use the seven-year mark as the time to

consider a dog a "senior." This term does not imply that the dog is geriatric and has begun to fail in mind and body. Aging is essentially a slowing process. Humans readily admit that they feel a difference in their activity level from age 20 to 30, and then from 30 to 40, etc. By treating the seven-year-old dog as a senior, owners are able to implement certain therapeutic and preventative medical strategies with the help of their vets.

A senior-care program should include at least two veterinary visits per year and screening sessions to determine the dog's health status, as well as nutritional counseling. Vets determine the senior dog's health status through a blood smear for a complete blood count, serum chemistry profile with electrolytes, urinalysis, blood pressure check, electrocardiogram, ocular tonometry (pressure on the eyeball) and dental prophylaxis.

Such an extensive program for senior dogs is well advised before owners start to see the obvious physical signs of aging, such as slower and inhibited movement, graying, increased sleep/nap periods and disinterest in play and other activity. This preventative program promises a longer, healthier life for the aging dog. Among the physical problems common in aging dogs are the loss of sight and hearing, arthritis, kidney and liver failure, diabetes mellitus, heart disease and Cushing's disease (a hormonal disease).

In addition to the physical manifestations discussed, there

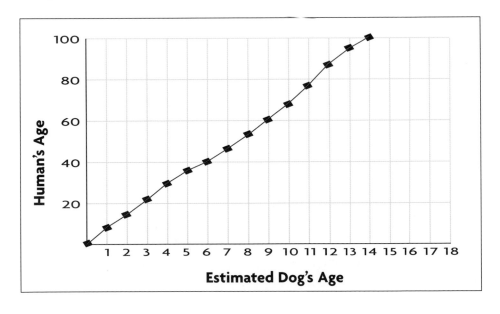

Blest with a hardy constitution, the Finnish Spitz approaches his senior years with vitality, as evidenced by this 11-year-old "youngster" who seems to say, "Me? A senior citizen? No way!"

are some behavioral changes and problems related to aging dogs. Dogs suffering from hearing or vision loss, dental discomfort or arthritis can become aggressive. Likewise, the near-deaf and/or blind dog may be startled more easily and react in an unexpectedly aggressive manner. Seniors suffering from senility can become more impatient and irritable. Housesoiling accidents are associated with loss of mobility, kidney problems and loss of sphincter control as well as plaque accumulation, physiological brain changes and reactions to medications. Older dogs, just like young puppies, suffer from separation anxiety, which can lead to excessive barking, whining, housesoiling and destructive behavior. Seniors may become fearful of everyday sounds, such as vacuum cleaners, heaters, thunder and passing traffic. Some dogs have difficulty sleeping, due to discomfort, the need for frequent toilet visits and the like.

Owners should avoid spoiling the older dog with too many treats. Obesity is a common problem in older dogs and subtracts years from their lives. Keep the senior dog as trim as possible, since excess weight puts additional stress on the body's vital organs. Some breeders recommend supplementing the diet with foods high in fiber and lower in calories. Adding fresh vegetables and marrow broth to the senior's diet makes a tasty, low-calorie, low-fat supplement. Vets also offer specialty diets for senior dogs that are worth exploring.

Your dog, as he nears his twilight years, needs your patience and good care more than ever. Never punish an older dog for an accident or abnormal behavior. For all the years of love, protection and companionship that your dog has provided, he deserves special attention and courtesies. The older dog may need to relieve himself at 3 a.m. because he can no longer "hold it" for eight hours. Older dogs may not be able to remain crated for more than two or three hours. It may be time to give up a sofa or chair to your old friend. Although he may not seem as enthusiastic about your attention and petting, he does appreciate the considerations you offer as he gets older.

Your Finnish Spitz does not understand why his world is slowing down. Owners must make their dogs' transition into the golden years as pleasant and rewarding as possible.

WHEN THE TIME COMES

You are never fully prepared to make a rational decision about putting your dog to sleep. It is very obvious that you love your Finnish Spitz or you would not be reading this book. Putting a beloved dog to sleep is extremely difficult. It is a decision that must be made with your vet. You are usually forced to make the decision when your dog experiences one or more life-threatening symptoms, requiring you to seek veterinary assistance. If the prognosis of the malady indicates that the end is near and that your beloved pet will only continue to suffer and experience no enjoyment for the balance of his life, then euthanasia is the right choice.

WHAT IS EUTHANASIA?

Euthanasia derives from the Greek, meaning "good death." In other words, it means the planned, painless killing of a dog suffering from a painful, incurable condition, or who is so aged that he cannot walk, see, eat or control his excretory functions. Euthanasia is usually accomplished by injection with an overdose of anesthesia or a barbiturate. Aside from the prick of the needle, the experience is usually painless.

MAKING THE DECISION

The decision to euthanize your dog is never easy. The days during which the dog becomes ill and the end occurs can be unusually stressful for you. If this is your first experience with the death of a loved one, you may need the

Cremation is an option for those who wish to memorialize their deceased pets. Cemeteries usually have areas in which to accommodate urns that contain the dogs' ashes.

comfort dictated by your religious beliefs. If you are the head of the family and have children, you should have involved them in the decision of putting your Finnish Spitz to sleep. Usually your dog can be maintained on drugs at the vet's clinic for a few days in order to give you ample time to make a decision. During this time, talking with members of your family or with people who have lived through the same experience can ease the burden of your inevitable decision.

THE FINAL RESTING PLACE

Dogs can have some of the same privileges as humans. The remains of your beloved dog can be buried in a pet cemetery, which is generally expensive. If your dog has died at home, he can be buried in your yard in a place suitably marked with a stone or a newly planted tree or bush. Alternatively, your dog can be cremated individually and the ashes returned to you. A less expensive option is

mass cremation, although, of course, the ashes of individual dogs cannot then be returned. Vets can usually help you locate a pet cemetery or arrange a cremation on your behalf if you choose one of these options. The costs should always be discussed frankly and openly with your vet.

GETTING ANOTHER DOG

The grief of losing your beloved dog will be as lasting as the grief of losing a human friend or relative. In most cases, if your dog died of old age (if there is such a thing), he had slowed down considerably. Do you want a new Finnish Spitz puppy to replace him? Or are you better off finding a more mature Finnish Spitz, say two to three years of age, which will usually be house-trained and will have an already developed personality. In this case, you can find out if you like each other after a few hours of being together.

The decision is, of course, your own. Do you want another Finnish Spitz or perhaps a different breed so as to avoid comparison with your beloved friend? Most people usually stay with the same breed because they know (and love) the characteristics of that breed. Then, too, they often know people who have the same breed and perhaps they are lucky enough that a breeder whom they know and respect expects a litter soon. What could be better?

BEHAVIOR OF YOUR
FINNISH SPITZ

THINK LIKE A DOG

Dogs do not think like humans, nor do humans think like dogs, though we try. Unfortunately, a dog is incapable of comprehending how humans think, so the responsibility falls on the owner to adopt a viable canine mindset. Dogs cannot rationalize, and they exist in the present moment. Many a dog owner makes the mistake in training of thinking that he can reprimand his dog for something that the dog did a while ago. Basically, you cannot even reprimand a dog for something he did 20 seconds ago! Either catch him in the act or forget it! It is a waste of your and your dog's time—in his mind, you are reprimanding him for whatever he is doing at that moment.

The following behavioral problems represent some which owners most commonly encounter. Every dog is unique and every situation is unique. No author could purport for you to solve your Finnish Spitz's problems simply by reading a chapter in a breed book. Here we outline some basic "dogspeak" so that owners' chances of solving behavioral problems are increased.

Discuss bad habits with your vet and he can recommend a behavioral specialist to consult in appropriate cases. Since behavioral abnormalities are the main reason for owners' abandoning their pets, we hope that you will make a valiant effort to solve your Finnish Spitz's problems. Patience and understanding are virtues that must dwell in every pet-loving household.

SEPARATION ANXIETY

Recognized by behaviorists as the most common form of stress for dogs, separation anxiety can also lead to destructive behaviors in your dog. It's more than your Finnish Spitz's howling his displeasure at your leaving the house and his being left alone. This is a normal reaction, no different than the child who cries as his mother leaves him on the first day at school. Separation anxiety is more serious. In fact, if you are constantly with your dog, he will come to expect you with him all of the time, making it even more traumatic for him when you are not there.

Obviously, you enjoy spending time with your dog, and he

> **I'M HOME!**
> Dogs left alone for varying lengths of time may often react wildly when their owners return. Sometimes they run, jump, bite, chew, tear things apart, wet themselves, gobble their food or behave in very undisciplined ways. If your dog behaves in this manner upon your return home, allow him to calm down before greeting him or he will consider your attention as a reward for his antics.

thrives on your love and attention. However, it should not become a dependent relationship in which he is heartbroken without you. This broken heart can also bring on destructive behavior as well as loss of appetite, depression and lack of interest in play and interaction. Canine behaviorists have been spending much time and energy to help owners better understand the significance of this stressful condition.

One thing you can do to minimize separation anxiety is to make your entrances and exits as low-key as possible. Do not give your dog a long drawn-out goodbye, and do not lavish him with hugs and kisses when you return. This is giving in to the attention that he craves, and it will only make him miss it more when you are away. Another thing you can try is to give your dog a treat when you leave; this will not only keep him occupied and keep his mind off the fact that you have just left but it also will also help him associate your leaving with a pleasant experience.

You may have to accustom your dog to being left alone at intervals. Of course, when your dog starts whimpering as you approach the door, your first instinct will be to run to him and comfort him, but do not do it! Eventually he will adjust to your absence. His anxiety stems from being placed in an unfamiliar situation; by familiarizing him with being alone, he will learn that he will survive. That is not to say you should purposely leave your dog home alone, but the dog needs to know that, while he can depend on you for his care, you do not have to be by his side 24 hours a day. Some behaviorists recommend tiring the dog out before you leave home—take him for a good long walk or engage in a game of fetch.

When the dog is alone in the house, he should be placed in his crate—another distinct advantage to crate training your dog. The crate should be placed in his familiar happy family area, where he normally sleeps and already feels comfortable, thereby making him feel more at ease when he is alone. Be sure to give the dog a special chew toy to enjoy while he settles into his crate.

AGGRESSION

Although the Finnish Spitz is not known as an aggressive breed, aggression is a problem that concerns all responsible dog owners. Aggression can be a very big problem in dogs, and, when not controlled, always becomes dangerous. An aggressive dog, no matter the size, may lunge at, bite or even attack a person or another dog. Aggressive behavior is not to be tolerated. It is more than just inappropriate behavior; it is painful for a family to watch its dog become unpredictable in his behavior to the point where they are afraid of him. While not all aggressive behavior is dangerous, behavior such as growling, baring teeth, etc., can be frightening. It is important to ascertain why the dog is acting in this manner. Aggression is a display of dominance, and the dog should not have the dominant role in his pack, which is, in this case, your family.

It is important not to challenge an aggressive dog, as this could provoke an attack. Observe your Finnish Spitz's body language. Does he make direct eye contact and stare? Does he try to make himself as large as possible: ears pricked, chest out, tail erect? Height and size signify authority in a dog pack—being taller or "above" another dog literally means that he is "above" in social status. These body signals tell you that your Finnish Spitz thinks he is in charge, a problem that needs to be addressed. An aggressive dog is unpredictable; you never know when he is going to strike and what he is going to do next. You cannot understand why a dog that is playful one minute is growling the next.

Fear is a common cause of aggression in dogs. Perhaps your

Finnish Spitz are generally non-aggressive with members of their own breed, especially when they live together. This group keeps a vigilant watch over their home and property.

Finnish Spitz had a negative experience as a puppy, which causes him to be fearful when a similar situation presents itself later in life. The dog may act aggressively in order to protect himself from whatever is making him afraid. It is not always easy to determine what is making your dog fearful, but if you can isolate what brings out the fear reaction, you can help the dog get over it.

Supervise your Finnish Spitz's interactions with people and other dogs, and praise the dog when it goes well. If he starts to act aggressively in a situation, correct him and remove him from the situation. Do not let people approach the dog and start petting him without your express permission. That way, you can have the dog sit to accept petting, and praise him when he behaves properly. You are focusing on praise and on modifying his behavior by rewarding him when he acts appropriately. By being gentle and by supervising his interactions, you are showing him that there is no need to be afraid or defensive.

The best solution is to consult a behavioral specialist, one who has experience with the Finnish Spitz or other spitz breeds if possible. Together, perhaps you can pinpoint the cause of your dog's aggression and do something about it. An aggressive dog cannot be trusted, and a dog that cannot be trusted is not safe to have as a family pet. If, very unusually, you find that your pet has become untrustworthy and you feel it necessary to seek a new home with a more suitable family and environment, explain fully to the new owners all your reasons for rehoming the dog to be fair to all concerned.

AGGRESSION TOWARD OTHER DOGS
A dog's aggressive behavior toward another dog stems from not enough exposure to other dogs at an early age. A male Finnish Spitz can be dominant and aggressive toward strange dogs, although they typically get along with other dogs in the home. However, if other dogs make your Finnish Spitz nervous and agitated, he will lash out as a protective mechanism. A dog that has not received sufficient exposure to other canines tends to think that he is the only dog on the planet. The animal becomes so dominant that he does not even show signs that he is fearful or threatened. Without growling or any other

---

TUG-OF-WAR
You should never play tug-of-war games with your puppy. Such games create a struggle for "top dog" position and teach the puppy that it is okay to challenge you. It will also encourage your puppy's natural tendency to bite down hard and *win*.

physical signal as a warning, he will lunge at and bite the other dog.

A way to correct this is to let your Finnish Spitz approach another dog when walking on lead. Watch very closely and, at the first sign of aggression, correct your Finnish Spitz and pull him away. Scold him for any sign of discomfort, and then praise him when he ignores the other dog. Keep this up until either he stops the aggressive behavior, learns to ignore other dogs or even accepts other dogs. Praise him lavishly for his correct behavior.

DOMINANT AGGRESSION

A social hierarchy is firmly established in a wild dog pack. The dog wants to dominate those under him and please those above him. Dogs know that there must be a leader. If you are not the obvious choice for emperor, the dog will assume the throne! These conflicting innate desires are what a dog owner is up against when he sets about training a dog. In training a dog to obey commands, the owner is reinforcing that he is the top dog in the "pack" and that the dog should, and should want to, serve his superior. Thus, the owner is suppressing the dog's urge to dominate by modifying his behavior and making him obey his owner, the pack leader.

An important part of training is taking every opportunity to

Play-fighting among dogs is normal canine behavior to establish dominance; this type of rough-housing should not be confused with aggression.

reinforce that you are the leader. The simple action of making your Finnish Spitz sit to wait for his food instead of allowing him to run up to get it when he wants it says that you control when he eats; he is dependent on you for food. Although it may be difficult, do not give in to your dog's wishes every time he whines at you or looks at you with pleading eyes. It is a constant effort to show the dog that his place in the pack is at the bottom.

This is not meant to sound cruel or inhumane. You love your Finnish Spitz and you should treat him with care and affection. Dog training is not about being cruel, it is about molding the dog's behavior into what is acceptable and teaching him to live by your rules. In theory, it is quite simple: catch him in appropriate behavior and reward him for it. Add a dog into the equation and it becomes a bit more trying, but, as a rule of thumb, positive reinforcement is what works best.

With a dominant dog, punishment and negative reinforcement can have the opposite effect of what you are after. It can make a dog fearful and/or act out aggressively if he feels he is being challenged. Remember, a dominant dog perceives himself at the top of the social heap, and will fight to defend his perceived status. The best way to prevent that is to never give him reason to think that he is in control in the first place.

If you are having trouble training your Finnish Spitz and it seems as if he is constantly challenging your authority, seek the help of an obedience trainer or behavioral specialist. A professional will work with both you and your dog to teach you effective techniques to use at home. Beware of trainers who rely on excessively harsh methods; scolding is necessary now and then, but the focus in your training should *always* be on positive reinforcement.

SEXUAL BEHAVIOR
Dogs exhibit certain sexual behaviors that may have influenced your choice of male or female when you first purchased your Finnish Spitz. To a certain extent, spaying/neutering will eliminate these behaviors, but if you are purchasing a dog that you wish to breed from, you should be aware of what you will have to deal with throughout the dog's life.

Female dogs usually have two estruses per year, with each season lasting about three weeks. These are the only times in which a female dog will mate, and she usually will not allow this until the second week of the cycle, although this varies from bitch to bitch. If not bred during the heat cycle, it is not uncommon for a bitch to experience a false pregnancy, in which her mammary glands swell and she exhibits maternal tendencies toward toys or other objects.

With male dogs, owners must be aware that whole dogs (dogs who are not neutered) have the natural inclination to mark their territory. Males mark their territory by spraying small amounts of urine as they lift their legs in a macho ritual. Marking can occur both outdoors in the yard and around the neighborhood as well as indoors on furniture legs, curtains and the sofa. Such behavior can be very frustrating for the owner; early training is strongly urged before the "urge" strikes your dog. Neutering the male at an appropriate early age can solve this problem before it becomes a habit.

Other problems associated with males are wandering and mounting. Both of these habits, of course, belong to the unneutered dog, whose sexual drive leads him away from home in search of the bitch in heat. Males will mount females in heat, as well as any other dog, male or female, that happens to catch their fancy. Other possible mounting partners include his owner, the furniture, guests to the home and strangers on the street. Discourage such behavior early on.

Owners must further recognize that mounting is not merely a sexual expression but also one of dominance, seen in males and females alike. Be consistent and be persistent, and you will find that you can "move mounters."

CHEWING

The national canine pastime is chewing! Every dog loves to sink his "canines" into a tasty bone, so it is important to provide your dog with appropriate chew toys so that he doesn't destroy your possessions or make a habit of nipping at your fingers and ankles. All dogs need to chew to massage their gums, to make their new teeth feel better and to exercise their jaws. This is a natural behavior that is deeply embedded in all things canine. Our role as owners is not to stop the dog's chewing, but rather to redirect it to positive, chew-worthy objects.

Be an informed owner and purchase proper chew toys, like strong nylon bones, that will not splinter. Be sure that the objects

A successful steal! This pup has made it back to his bed with a tasty sock on which to chew, likely to the dismay of his owner.

are safe and durable, since your dog's safety is at risk. Again, the owner is responsible for ensuring a dog-proof environment.

The best answer is prevention; that is, put your shoes, handbags and other tasty objects in their proper places (out of the reach of the growing canine mouth). Direct your puppy to his toys whenever you see him "tasting" the furniture legs or the leg of your pants. Make a loud noise to attract the pup's attention and immediately escort him to his chew toy and engage him with the toy for at least four minutes, praising and encouraging him all the while. An array of safe, interesting chew toys will keep your dog's mind and teeth occupied, and distracted from chewing on things he shouldn't.

Some trainers recommend deterrents, such as hot pepper, a bitter spice or a product designed for this purpose, to discourage the dog from chewing on unwanted objects. Test these products to see which works best before investing in large quantities.

JUMPING UP

Jumping up is a dog's friendly way of saying hello! Some dog owners do not mind when their dog jumps up. The problem arises when guests come to the house and the dog greets them in the same manner—whether they like it or not! However friendly the greeting may be, the chances are that your visitors will not appreciate your dog's enthusiasm. The dog will not be able to distinguish upon whom he can jump and whom he cannot. Therefore, it is probably best to discourage this behavior entirely.

Pick a command such as "Off" (avoid using "Down" since you will use that for the dog to lie down) and tell him "Off" when he jumps up. Place him on the ground on all fours and have him sit, praising him the whole time. Always lavish him with praise and petting when he is in the sit position. In this way, you can give him a warm affectionate greeting, let him know that you are as excited to see him as he is to see you and instill good manners at the same time!

DIGGING

Digging, which is seen as a destructive behavior to humans, is actually quite a natural behavior in dogs. Although terriers (aptly known as the "earth dogs") are most associated with digging, any dog's desire to dig can be irrepressible and most frustrating to his owners. When digging occurs in your yard, it is actually a normal behavior redirected into something the dog can do in his everyday life. In the wild, a dog would be actively seeking food, making his own shelter, etc. He would be using his paws in a purposeful manner for his survival. Since you provide him with food and shelter, he has no need to use his paws for these purposes, and so the energy that he would be using may manifest itself in the form of little holes all over your yard and flower beds.

Perhaps your dog is digging as a reaction to boredom—it is somewhat similar to someone eating a whole bag of chips in front of the TV—because they are there and there is nothing better to do! Basically, the answer is to provide the dog with adequate play and exercise so that his mind and paws are occupied, and so that he feels as if he is doing something useful.

Of course, digging is easiest to control if it is stopped as soon as possible, but it is often hard to catch a dog in the act. If your dog is a compulsive digger and is not easily distracted by other activities, you can designate an area on your property where he is allowed to dig. If you catch him digging in an off-limits area, immediately take him to the approved area and praise him for digging there. Keep a close eye on him so that you can catch him in the act—that is the only way to make him understand what is permitted and what is not. If you take him to a hole he dug an hour ago and tell him "No," he will understand that you are not fond of holes, dirt or flowers. If you catch him while he is stifle-deep in your tulips, that is when he will get your message.

BARKING

Dogs cannot talk—oh, what they would say if they could! Instead, barking is a dog's way of "talking." It can be somewhat frustrating because it is not always easy to tell what a dog means by his bark—is he excited, happy, frightened or angry? Whatever it is that the dog is trying to say, he should not be punished for barking. It is only when the barking becomes excessive, and when the excessive barking becomes a bad habit, that the behavior needs to be modified.

Finnish Spitzen are highly vocal dogs. They bark rapidly while hunting and bark to alert their owners to things. For example, if an intruder came into your home in the middle of the night and your Finnish Spitz barked a warning, wouldn't you be

Finnish Spitzen certainly have a lot to say! This is a vocal breed, something that should not be overlooked in your decision to own a Finnish Spitz.

pleased? You would probably deem your dog a hero, a wonderful guardian and protector of the home. On the other hand, if a friend drops by unexpectedly, rings the doorbell and is greeted with a sudden sharp bark, you would probably be annoyed at the dog. But in reality, isn't this just the same behavior? The dog does not know any better. Unless he sees who is at the door and it is someone he knows, he will bark as a means of vocalizing that his (and your) territory is being threatened. While your friend is not posing a threat, it is all the same to the dog. Barking is his means of letting you know that there is an intrusion, whether friend or foe, on your property. This type of barking is instinctive and should not be discouraged.

Excessive habitual barking, however, is a problem that should be corrected early on. As your Finnish Spitz grows up, you will be able to tell when his barking is purposeful and when it is for no reason. You will become able to distinguish your dog's different barks and their meanings. For example, the bark when someone comes to the door will be different than the bark when he is excited to see you. It is similar to a person's tone of voice, except that the dog has to rely totally on tone of voice because he does not have the benefit of using words. An incessant barker will be evident at an early age.

There are some things that encourage a dog to bark. For example, if your dog barks non-stop for a few minutes and you give him a treat to quiet him, he believes that you are rewarding him for barking. He will associate barking with getting a treat and will keep doing it until he is rewarded. On the other hand, if you give him a command such as "Quiet" and praise him after he has stopped barking for a few seconds, he will get the idea that being "quiet" is what you want him to do.

FOOD STEALING
Is your dog devising ways of stealing food from your coffee table or kitchen counter? If so, you must answer the following questions: Is your Finnish Spitz hungry or is he "constantly famished" like many dogs seem to be? Face it, some dogs are more food-motivated than others. They are totally obsessed by the smell of food and can only think of their next meal.

Food stealing is terrific fun and always yields a great reward—*food*, glorious food.

Your goal as an owner, therefore, is to be sensible about where food is placed in the home and to reprimand your dog whenever he is caught in the act of stealing. But remember, only reprimand your dog if you actually see him stealing, not later when the crime is discovered; that will be of no use at all and will only serve to confuse him.

BEGGING
Just like food stealing, begging is a favorite pastime of hungry puppies! It achieves that same wonderful result—*food!* Dogs quickly learn that their owners keep the "good food" for themselves, and that we humans do not dine on kibble alone. Begging is a conditioned response related to a specific stimulus, time and place. The sounds of the kitchen, cans and bottles opening, crinkling bags, the smell of food in preparation, etc., will excite the dog, and soon the paws will be in the air!

Here is the solution to stopping this behavior: Never give in to a beggar! You are rewarding the dog for sitting pretty, jumping up, whining and rubbing his nose into you by giving him food. By ignoring the dog, you will (eventually) force the behavior into extinction. Note that the behavior is likely to get worse before it disappears, so be sure there are not any "softies" in the family who will give in to little "Oliver" every time he whimpers, "More, please."

COPROPHAGIA

Feces eating is, to humans, one of the most disgusting behaviors that our dogs could engage in; yet, to dogs, it is perfectly normal. It is hard for us to understand why a dog would want to eat his own feces (or those of another animal). He could be seeking certain nutrients that are missing from his diet, he could be just hungry or he could be attracted by the pleasing (to a dog) scent.

Vets have found that diets with low levels of digestibility, containing relatively low levels of fiber and high levels of starch, increase coprophagia. Therefore, high-fiber diets may decrease the likelihood of dogs' eating feces. Both the consistency of the stool (how firm it feels in the dog's mouth) and the presence of undigested nutrients increase the likelihood. Thus, once the dog develops diarrhea from feces eating, he will likely stop this distasteful habit.

To discourage this behavior, first make sure that the food you are feeding your dog is nutritionally complete and that he is getting enough food. If changes in his diet do not seem to work, and no medical cause can be found, you will have to modify the

Meal time can be practice time. Having the dog sit and stay while he waits for your "OK" to eat reinforces the basic commands and encourages polite behavior where food is concerned.

behavior through environmental control before it becomes a habit. The best way to prevent your dog from eating his stool is to make it unavailable—clean up after he eliminates and remove any stool from the yard. If it is not there, he cannot eat it.

Reprimanding for stool eating rarely impresses the dog. Vets recommend distracting the dog while he is in the act of stool eating. Coprophagia is seen most frequently in pups 6 to 12 months of age, and usually disappears around the dog's first birthday.

FINNISH SPITZ

When you purchase your Finnish Spitz, you will make it clear to the breeder whether you want one just as a lovable companion and pet, or if you hope to be buying a Finnish Spitz with show prospects. No reputable breeder will sell you a young puppy and tell you that it is *definitely* of show quality, for so much can go wrong during the early months of a puppy's development. If you plan to show, what you will hopefully have acquired is a puppy with "show potential."

To the novice, exhibiting a Finnish Spitz in the show ring may look easy, but it takes a lot of hard work and devotion to do top winning at a show such as the prestigious Westminster Kennel Club dog show, not to mention a little luck too!

The first concept that the

canine novice learns when watching a dog show is that each dog first competes against members of his own breed. Once the judge has selected the best member of each breed (Best of Breed), provided that the show is judged on a Group system, that chosen dog will compete with other dogs in his group. Finally, the dogs chosen first in each group will compete for Best in Show.

The second concept that you must understand is that the dogs are not actually compared against one another. The judge compares each dog against his breed standard, the written description of the ideal specimen that is approved by the American Kennel Club (AKC). While some early breed standards were indeed based on specific dogs that were famous or popular, many dedicated enthusiasts say that a perfect specimen, as described in the standard, has never walked into a show ring, has never been bred and, to the woe of dog breeders around the globe, does not exist.

If you are interested in exploring the world of dog showing, your best bet is to join your local

AKC GROUPS

For showing purposes, the American Kennel Club divides its recognized breeds into seven groups: Sporting Dogs, Hounds, Working Dogs, Terriers, Toys, Non-Sporting Dogs and Herding Dogs. The Finnish Spitz competes in the Non-Sporting Group.

Concentration is intense in the show ring. Look at the dog's gaze focused on his handler, keeping steady eye contact as he stands at attention to look his best for the judge.

breed club or the national club, which is the Finnish Spitz Club of America (www.finnishspitzclub.org). These clubs often host both regional and national specialties, shows only for Finnish Spitzen, which can include conformation as well as obedience, agility and other types of trials. Even if you have no intention of competing with your Finnish Spitz, a specialty is like a festival for lovers of the breed who congregate to share their favorite topic: the Finnish Spitz! Clubs also send out newsletters, and some organize training days and seminars in order that people may learn more about their chosen breed.

To locate the breed club closest to you, contact the American Kennel Club, which furnishes the rules and regulations for all of these events plus general dog registration and other basic requirements of dog ownership. In the US, the American Kennel Club offers three kinds of conformation shows: an all-breed show (for all AKC-recognized breeds); a specialty show (for one breed only, usually sponsored by the parent club); and a Group show (for all breeds in the group).

For a dog to become an AKC champion of record, the dog must accumulate 15 points at the shows from at least three different judges, including two "majors." A "major" is defined as a three-, four- or five-point win, and the number of

points per win is determined by the number of dogs entered in the show on that day. Depending on the breed, the number of points that are awarded varies. With more popular breeds, more dogs are needed to rack up the points; the opposite is true for those breeds that are less numerous (like the Finnish Spitz).

At any dog show, only one dog and one bitch of each breed can win points. Dog showing does not offer "co-ed" classes. Dogs and bitches never compete against each other in the classes. Non-champion dogs are called "class dogs" because they compete in one of the five classes. Dogs are entered in a particular class depending on age and previous show wins. To begin, there is the Puppy Class (for 6- to 9-month-olds and for 9- to 12-month-olds); this class is followed by the Novice Class (for dogs that have not won any first prizes except in the Puppy Class nor three first prizes in the Novice Class and have not accumulated any points toward their champion title); the Bred-by-Exhibitor Class (for dogs handled by their breeders or by one of the breeder's immediate family); the American-bred Class (for dogs bred in the US!); and the Open Class (for any dog that is not a champion).

The judge at the show begins judging the Puppy Class, first dogs and then bitches, and proceeds through the classes. The judge places his winners first through fourth in each class. In the Winners Class, the first-place winners of each class compete with one another to determine Winners Dog and Winners Bitch. The judge also places a Reserve Winners Dog and Reserve Winners Bitch, which could be awarded the points in the case of a disqualification. The Winners Dog and Winners Bitch, the two that are awarded the points for the breed, then compete with any champions of record entered in the show, usually called "specials." The judge reviews the Winners Dog, Winners Bitch and all of the specials to select his Best of Breed. The Best of Winners is selected between the Winners Dog and Winners Bitch. Were one of these two to be selected Best of Breed, he or she would automatically be named Best of Winners as well. Finally the judge selects his Best of Opposite Sex to the Best of Breed winner.

At a Group show or all-breed show, the Best of Breed winners from each breed then compete against one another for Group One through Group Four. The judge compares each Best of Breed to his breed standard, and the dog that most closely lives up to the ideal for his breed is selected as Group One. Finally, all seven group winners (from the Non-Sporting Group, Toy Group, Hound Group, etc.) compete for Best in Show.

KENNEL CLUB CONTACTS
You can get information about dog shows from the national kennel clubs:

American Kennel Club
5580 Centerview Dr., Raleigh, NC 27606-3390
www.akc.org

United Kennel Club
100 E. Kilgore Road, Kalamazoo, MI 49002
www.ukcdogs.com

Canadian Kennel Club
89 Skyway Ave., Suite 100, Etobicoke, Ontario M9W 6R4, Canada
www.ckc.ca

The Kennel Club
1-5 Clarges St., Piccadilly, London W1Y 8AB, UK
www.the-kennel-club.org.uk

Fédération Cynologique Internationale
14, rue Leopold II, B-6530 Thuin, Belgium
www.fci.be

ENTERING A SHOW

To find out about dog shows in your area, you can subscribe to the American Kennel Club's monthly magazine, the *American Kennel Gazette* and the accompanying *Events Calendar*. You can also look in your local newspaper for advertisements for dog shows in your area or go on the Internet to the AKC's website, http:www.akc.org.

If your Finnish Spitz is six months of age or older and registered with the AKC, you can enter him in a dog show where the breed is offered classes. Provided that your Finnish Spitz does not have a disqualifying fault, he can compete. Only unaltered dogs can be entered in a dog show, so if you have spayed or neutered your Finnish Spitz, you cannot compete in conformation shows. The reason for this is simple. Dog shows are the main forum to prove which representatives in a breed are worthy of being bred. Only dogs that have achieved championships—the AKC "seal of approval" for quality in pure-bred dogs—should be bred. Altered dogs, however, can participate in other AKC events such as obedience trials and the Canine Good Citizen® program.

Before you actually step into the ring, you would be well advised to sit back and observe the judge's ring procedure. If it is your first time in the ring, do not be over-anxious and run to the front of the line. It is much better to stand back and study how the exhibitor in front of you is performing. The judge asks each handler to stand or "stack" the dog, hopefully showing the dog off to his best advantage. The judge will observe the dog from a distance and from different angles, and approach the dog to check his teeth, overall structure, alertness and muscle tone, as well as consider how well the dog "conforms" to the standard. Most importantly, the judge will have the exhibitor move the dog around the ring in some pattern that he should specify (another advantage to not going first, but always listen since some judges change their directions—and the judge is always right!). Finally, the judge will give the dog one last look before moving on to the next exhibitor.

If you are not in the top four in your class at your first show, do not be discouraged. Be patient and consistent, and you may eventually find yourself in a winning line-up. Remember that the winners were once in your shoes and have devoted many hours and much money to earn the placement. If you find that your dog is losing every time and never getting a nod, it may be time to consider a different dog sport or to just enjoy your Finnish Spitz as a pet. Parent clubs offer other events, such as agility, tracking, obedience, instinct tests and more, which may be of interest to the owner of a well-trained Finnish Spitz.

OBEDIENCE TRIALS
Obedience trials in the US trace back to the early 1930s when organized obedience training was developed to demonstrate how well dog and owner could work together. The pioneer of obedience trials is Mrs. Helen Whitehouse Walker, a Standard Poodle fancier, who designed a series of exercises after the Associated Sheep, Police Army Dog Society of Great Britain. Since the days of Mrs. Walker, obedience trials have grown by leaps and bounds, and today there are over 2,000 trials held in the US every year, with more than 100,000 dogs competing. Any AKC-registered dog can enter an obedience trial, regardless of conformational disqualifications or neutering.

Obedience trials are divided into three levels of progressive difficulty. At the first level, the Novice, dogs compete for the title Companion Dog (CD); at the intermediate level, the Open, dogs compete for the title Companion Dog Excellent (CDX); and at the advanced level, the Utility, dogs compete for the title Utility Dog (UD). Classes are sub-divided into "A" (for beginners) and "B" (for more experienced handlers). A

perfect score at any level is 200, and a dog must score 170 or better to earn a "leg," of which three are needed to earn the title. To earn points, the dog must score more than 50% of the available points in each exercise; the possible points range from 20 to 40.

Each level consists of a different set of exercises. In the Novice level, the dog must heel on- and off-lead, come, long sit, long down and stand for examination. These skills are the basic ones required for a well-behaved "Companion Dog." The Open level requires that the dog perform the same exer-

Though no longer common in the US, a bench show proves to be an educational experience for interested visitors. The benching area is like a "backstage" where the dogs must wait until their turn in the ring.

cises mentioned but without a leash for extended lengths of time, as well as retrieve a dumbbell, broad jump and drop on recall. In the Utility level, dogs must perform ten difficult exercises, including scent discrimination, hand signals for basic commands, directed jump and directed retrieve.

Once a dog has earned the UD title, he can compete with other proven obedience dogs for the coveted title Utility Dog Excellent (UDX), which requires that the dog win "legs" in ten shows. Utility Dogs who earn "legs" in Open B and Utility B earn points toward their Obedience Trial Champion title. In 1977, the title Obedience Trial Champion (OTCh.) was established by the AKC. To become an OTCh., a dog needs to earn 100 points, which requires three first places in Open B and Utility under three different judges.

The Grand Prix of obedience trials, the AKC National Obedience Invitational gives qualifying Utility Dogs the chance to win the newest and highest title: National Obedience Champion (NOC). Only the top 25 ranked obedience dogs, plus any dog ranked in the top 3 in his breed, are allowed to compete.

AGILITY TRIALS
Having had its origins in the UK back in 1977, AKC agility had its official beginning in the US in August 1994, when the first licensed agility trials were held. The AKC allows all registered breeds (including Miscellaneous Class breeds) to participate, providing the dog is 12 months of age or older. Agility is designed so that the handler demonstrates how well the dog can work at his side. The handler directs his dog over an obstacle course that includes jumps as well as tires, the dog walk, weave poles, pipe tunnels, collapsed tunnels, etc. While working his way through the course, the dog must keep one eye and ear on the handler and the rest of his body on the course. The handler gives verbal and hand signals to guide the dog through the course.

The first organization to promote agility trials in the US was the United States Dog Agility Association, Inc. (USDAA), which was established in 1986 and spawned numerous member clubs around the country. Both the

---

TEMPERAMENT PLUS
Although it seems that physical conformation is the only factor considered in the show ring, temperament is also of utmost importance. An aggressive or fearful dog should not be shown, as bad behavior will not be tolerated and may pose a threat to the judge, other exhibitors, you and your dog.

USDAA and the AKC offer titles to winning dogs. Three titles are available through the USDAA: Agility Dog (AD), Advanced Agility Dog (AAD) and Master Agility Dog (MAD). The AKC offers Novice Agility (NA), Open Agility (OA), Agility Excellent (AX) and Master Agility Excellent (MX). Beyond these four AKC titles, dogs can win additional ones in "jumper" classes, Jumpers with Weave Novice (NAJ), Open (OAJ) and Excellent (MXJ), which lead to the ultimate title(s): MACH, Master Agility Champion. Dogs can continue to add number designations to the MACH titles, indicating how many times the dog has met the MACH requirements, such as MACH1, MACH2, and so on.

Agility is great fun for dog and owner with many rewards for everyone involved. Interested owners should join a training club that has obstacles and experienced agility handlers who can introduce you and your dog to the "ropes" (and tires, tunnels, etc.).

TRACKING

Any dog is capable of tracking, using his nose to follow a trail. Tracking tests are exciting and competitive ways to test your Finnish Spitz's scenting ability. The AKC started tracking tests in 1937, when the first AKC-licensed test took place as a part of the Utility level at an obedience trial.

The judge poses with the day's proud winners and handlers.

Ten years later in 1947, the AKC offered the first title, Tracking Dog (TD). It was not until 1980 that the AKC added the title Tracking Dog Excellent (TDX), which was followed by the title Versatile Surface Tracking (VST) in 1995. The title Champion Tracker (CT) is awarded to a dog who has earned all three titles

In the beginning level of tracking, the owner follows the dog through a field on a long leash. To earn the TD title, the dog must follow a track laid by a human 30 to 120 minutes prior. The track is about 500 yards long with up to 5 directional changes. The TDX requires that the dog follow a track that is 3 to 5 hours old over a course up to 1,000 yards long with up to 7 directional changes. The VST requires that the dog follow a track up to five hours old through an urban setting.

INDEX

My Finnish Spitz

PUT YOUR PUPPY'S FIRST PICTURE HERE

Dog's Name _____

Date _____ Photographer _____